Me and My Mum

BY

GRACE CHAMA-PUPE

Me and MY MUM

Order this book online at www.trafford.com
or email orders@trafford.com

Most Trafford titles are also available at major online book retailers.

Printed in the United States of America.

ISBN: 978-1-4669-4393-3 (sc)
ISBN: 978-1-4669-4392-6 (e)

Trafford rev. 09/07/2012

 www.trafford.com

North America & international
toll-free: 1 888 232 4444 (USA & Canada)
phone: 250 383 6864 ✦ fax: 812 355 4082

CONTENTS

ACKNOWLEDGEMENT

To the memory of my late father Mr Jairous Chama Katebe who gave me a 'jump start' to a life he never lived long enough to witness. To my mother, Besa Milika Mulutula who is currently engulfed in turmoil as she journeys in her last twilight days savaged by on-set dementia. A big thank you to the people I spoke to about writing this book who gave me tremendous encouragement even though they were mostly strangers. And a big thank you to my publishers 'Traffords' who accepted work from a novice author with such enthusiasm.

ME, MUM AND HER ON-SET DEMENTIA

What is dementia?

According to an article written by (GC Roman—Journal of the American Geriatrics Society 2003—Wiley on line library) dementia is described as a loss of brain functions that occurs with certain diseases in the elderly. Illnesses may include: Alzheimer's disease, vascular dementia, Parkinson's, Huntingdon's disease, alcohol-related dementia, AIDS related dementia and Creutzfieldt—Jacob disease.

The article further states that Vascular dementia (CVD) is the second most common cause of dementia in the elderly.

What is vascular dementia?

It is the loss of cognitive functioning resulting from ischemic, hypo perfusive, or hemorrhagic brain lesions due to cerebral vascular disease. Symptoms of vascular dementia are a 'stepped' progression with symptoms remaining at a constant level for a time and then suddenly deteriorating.

It is stated that people with dementia may particularly experience: Problems with speed thinking; concentration and communication; depression and anxiety accompanying the dementia; symptoms of stroke, such as physical weakness or paralysis; memory loss; seizures and periods of severe or acute confusion. Other symptoms may include: visual mistakes and misperceptions; changes in behaviour such as restlessness; difficulties with walking and steadiness; hallucinations (seeing or hearing things that aren't there) and delusions (believing things that are not true). Problems with continence as well as psychological symptoms such as becoming more obsessive.

At the time of writing this book, my mum had not officially been diagnosed as suffering from dementia as I was still in the process of finding a sympathetic specialist doctor in Zambia who may not dismiss mum's ailments as simply old age degeneration.

However, my mother who is aged 89 has been expressing symptoms of on set dementia which include forgetfulness, confusion, misperceptions, behavioural difficulties, hallucinations as well as becoming more obsessive.

My mother like many other elderly people in Zambia who are at the brink of enduring early onset dementia and those already suffering from dementia have no voice to tell the world and let alone their own government about their dire twilight end to their lives. There are no organised lobbies to take up their pleas into, for example, parliamentary debates. Nobody is fighting for their quotas at government level. It seems to me that dementia is still regarded as a taboo subject which should not be debated openly hence mental health problems in the elderly has not received any publicity at government level.

Having spent my adult life living and working as a Social Worker in United Kingdom, I am at pains to witness the suffering and frustration of dementia sufferers as well as those trying to care for them in Zambian communities. It seems to me that caring responsibilities have been left on the mercy of various churches, families and some volunteers who provide assistance to the undeserving and other categories relying at the fledges of society. For example, in the worst case scenarios, the elderly, mentally ill and people with disabilities are left to roam streets and fend for themselves.

However, it is mostly stated that mental and physical health ailments which affect elderly people such as dementia, manic depression, psychosis, diabetes, high/low blood pressure to mention a few have no class nor creed hence today's leaders may find themselves in their old age faced with fragmented and broken down health care schemes unless they put their house in order and improve health care frame works in Zambia now, they may find themselves enduring the same hardships as today's elderly people.

On my return back to my native country, Zambia, I found myself thrown at the deepest end as I embarked on caring for my elderly mother who was expressing symptoms of on-set dementia. Little did I know that mum's 24/7 caring role will entirely be left on my two shoulders without any assistance from either family or government. The entire saga blew my breath away and left me drained and frustrated.

It goes without saying that when one door closes, the other one opens hence my dire frustration has resulted in writing a book based on my own personal experiences with mum, an on-set dementia sufferer. Observing and writing down my encounters with mum changed my negative feelings into positive ones as I became more and more interested in mum's activities both good and bad. It has also brought me closer to appreciating the mother I had before her on-set dementia.

MUM'S ARRIVAL

AFTER WEEKS OF NEGOTIATIONS, DELIBERATIONS and unexpected pros and cons into having mum brought to Lusaka, I finally sent my niece Anne to go and fetch mum from Chililabombwe. Their travel proves to be successful and on Saturday evening, 30th July, 2011 mum and Anne arrive in Lusaka. I instruct Anne to catch a taxi from Lusaka's City Bus Terminal to my home in Makeni as driving there meant having the two waiting for me. Within twenty minutes or so the taxi arrives at my house.

My first impressions were that mum appeared tired and disorientated. She looked extremely thin and I worried she might not be well hence she may need immediate medical health checks. She recognises me and on the whole she seems confused in this strange empty house. This was before the arrival of my household goods. The only furniture I had was a double bed in my bedroom, a three quarter bed in mum's room, a small cooker, small fridge and a leather stool.

I am anxious that mum might not take to my lonely life as she is used to living in households full of people. I am trying to make conversation with mum and she appears to having difficulties in retaining information and I quickly switch to simple chat about her ailments which she seems to like and tells me about her aches and pains.

I hastily prepare a bath for mum. I lace a half full bath tub with nice smelling foam bath and lead mum to the bathroom. I help her to undress and assist her to get in the bath. I feel happy that at least mum is mobile as long as she uses her walking stick, she is able to walk independently. I leave mum to soak her tired bones and close the door behind me after giving her strict instructions not to try to lie down in the bath tub. I purposely pause outside the bathroom door and carefully eardrop to what is going on inside the bathroom. Within seconds, I hear some chanting noises coming from the inside. I hold my breath as I try to make sense of what I am hearing. My heart is doing its sauna sets and my mouth is getting dry. I am thinking, is mum drowning, is she crying? What the hell is going on there? Before I know I knock on the door and burst in. I hesitantly stand over her and ask as to what is going on. "Mayo cinshi" (What is going on mum?) Mum looks up and says "Ndepepa" (I am praying).

I quickly apologize to her and leave so as to accord her privacy and allow her to continue with her prayers. Whilst outside, I am puzzled and astonished because I have never known my mum to be a religious fanatic. I know my parents belonged to Jehovah Witness and most of their prayers were very conservative and not openly expressed. Then I remember my mother once telling me many years ago that she now belongs to the Seventh Day Adventist Church. So I am partially amused and sorrowful. Amused in that I have never heard of anybody praying before taking a bath or could it be argued that Jesus Christ prayed before taking a bath in the River Jordan. But then, was that not for Baptism purposes? On the other hand, I am sorrowful in that I am not sure why mum should be praying. Is it that she feels safe and happier in the new environment or she is praying to thank God for her safe arrival. Well, whatever the case mum has just given me the first shock and probably I should be ready for more as I start a new life caring for her.

Afterwards, mum calls out that she is ready to come out of the bath tub, I rush back in the bathroom and assist her getting out and drying up. I lead her back in her bedroom still wrapped in a towel. When she sits on her bed, she looks at me and says "Ninshi ushaishile nsendela kale" (Why didn't you come to pick me up earlier). Mum's sentiments brings a lump in my throat. I sit down on her bed and say, mum my sister also tried to look after you as best as she could and besides I live abroad. It was difficult for me to live with you. Now that I am back home, we will live together in this empty house. Mum smiles. I feel good and proceed to dress her in a night dress.

I am wondering as to what light meal to prepare for mum. I know she will not want nshima as she is very tired. I make up my mind and boil some custard porridge for her. I bring a bowl of custard to her. Then I remember some wise words, I heard on BBC World News which says "Even an old cat drinks milk". I go back in the kitchen and boil some milk for mum. She seems to like custard which she washes down with hot milk. This marked the start of mum's liking for custard porridge. She could refuse all the meals but would accept a bowl of custard at any time of the day.

Mum spends the night peacefully and it was all smiles the following morning I carry on with familiarising mum to her new environments. Mum was surprised that I live in a house without any furniture. In her own words she says, "Inga ifipe fyamung'anda fili kwii?" (Where are your household goods?) I try to explain to mum that all my goods are in England and that I will have to go back and pack them up into a container and ship them to Zambia. This explanation is probably too complicated for mum to comprehend and she gazes ahead of her and asks no more questions.

With hind sight, I had no clue that by inviting mum into my house, I had just written off all my possessions, my wants and wishes to her, as on her bad days I am mistaken for her domestic servant.

THE WAKE UP CALL

Mayooo, Nachelomu, eeeh! Eeeeh!

I hastily sit up in bed. I gaze at my bedside clock—it is 5.20 am. I smile to myself. I am having a funny dream. I am with friends trying to cross over wide, fast-flowing and deep waters. Apparently, we are having difficulties because we cannot speak nor understand the language. I am telling my friends, "Let's use sign language otherwise we won't cross over". Cross over where? I say loudly to myself as I sit up with my heart throbbing in my mouth. I am thinking am I on holiday? Who are those friends? Before I even come to terms with visualising which river we are trying to cross, I sadly realise that I am just having a dream. Then suddenly another piercing call comes through. Mayoo, nachelume eeeh mayo nafwa ine! My instinct tells me something is seriously wrong with mum. I jump out off bed and run to her room.

Mum is in a sitting position her hands are clinched on her walking stick as though she wants to stand up. She falls back probably being disrupted by my sudden entry into her room.

I go and sit by her side and say "mayo cishi, namulwala?" (what's the matter mum, are you not well). Mum goes "inga akasalu kandi akabuta kali kwii?" (Where is my white cloth?) I swallow hard to conceal my rising anger. I am fuming to think the wailings from mum were about a misplaced flannel. Who does she think I am. Does she even care whether I am asleep or not? Which white cloth is she looking for?

In fact she hasn't got a white cloth the flannel I have given her to wipe her mouth while eating or wipe sweat from her face has green, red and yellow stripes. Before I even answer her back I look around for the flannel and there! It is neatly folded on her pillow. I say to her, mum the flannel is on your pillow (aka salu kali pa pillow) Mum shrugs in her sitting position and says "Nshacikamona" (I did not see it). I'm thinking for goodness sake, I am waiting for an apology from you. This never came. Mum changes the subject almost immediately and says "lelo nshilelepo fye nangu kamo" (to night I did not sleep even a little bit). I say, ooh, mum maybe it is because it was raining and you must have been disturbed by thunder and lightening. "Awe nshyacumfwa infula nangu panono". Mum goes, no, I did not hear the rain I did not even know there was a thunderstorm. And I am thinking—poor mum, she must have been fast asleep and yet she claims to have been awake all night. I kept my thoughts to myself and never challenged her. I responded by urging mum to get back to bed which she obediently obliged to do.

Not one to be challenged mum goes "Mwebantu ndeteleniko utumenshi twakunwa" (can anybody bring me a little water to drink) I feel angry and I say to her, how many times have I told you not to use incriminating language? You talk as though anybody has refused to give you water. Mum keeps quiet. I swallow hard and I feel guilty for raising my voice at her. In mum's mind-set there is no, "sorry", "thank you", "please" "excuse me" or "pardon me", these are small things I wish she may be accustomed to. Or am I asking for too much from her. Then a thought crops up in my head and I ask myself, "Is this woman I am caring for my mum? If so, why has her temperaments changed so much? My old mum was very kind, pleasant, very quiet and extremely fun. I used to share secrets with my mum. Illiterate as she was, mum used to give me the best advice I could ever get on earth.

I remember flying all the way from England many years ago just to come and sought mum's advice on my persistent marital problems. I flew to Lusaka and after a day or two, I caught a coach to Mansa. I rang mum while in Lusaka and as usual her first question was: Have you come with my son in-law? (Mwishile na batata?) I said, no mum, I am on my own. There was this little secret between us when I travel alone, mum moves in with me in Mansa Hotel where I usually booked. Mum loved moving to the Hotel where I could spoil her to bits. And besides that's where we used to hold our summits without any disturbance from relatives nor neighbours. Mum wanted to have quality time with me and used to hate the presence of others. So, when my financial status slightly improved, and to please my mum whom I have always felt missed on even a basic luxury life, I could book at the hotel and invite her to move in with me. This became her best time of her life. She once commented to me whilst at the hotel that she felt like a white woman (Nde umfwa kwati ndi missis) and I proudly said to her "Yes mum, you will be a madam for a week" and we both burst out laughing.

Our marital summit took two nights without a proper resolve. Mum kept saying "Awee ine ulya tata Kaonde nalimutemwa sana" (I Love my Kaonde son in-law) I could say to mum, yes he is a very nice kind man but there are certain inappropriate things which he does which are detrimental to a marriage. In the end I took on mum's advice and I was able to finally make up my mind. I will always be indebted to mum's wisdom and her precious talent to keep one sibling's secret. Remember there were six of us (siblings) but I have never heard any of them repeat the secrets I shared with mum to me. My mum was my anchor. And in later years when that pillar disappeared through mum's old age and her on set of dementia I have despaired as there has never been a confident ant replacement in my life.

Are there no sibling jealousies in other families? The desire to do better than others! Allow me to use this ananology to get this point clear. How can for example, a sibling compete on the road with another, who is driving a BMW or Pajero car to Kitwe when s/he is driving a Fiat Uno car? Can't s/he just ask for a lift from BMW/Pajero driver or let alone fly to Ndola and thereafter drive the Fiat Uno into Kitwe and cleverly win the race, though at a cost. There is a saying in English which goes "If you cannot win or defeat them, you join them". I like the Bemba saying which goes "Ukupoka icinsenda ku nkoko kunakilila". If only we can learn from these simple idioms I am sure there could be harmony in families rather than throwing vile at each other leading to unceasing rivalries.

I have always blamed dementia or on set of dementia which I feel has stolen my mother from me. I sometimes feel I am living with a stranger. My fun loving mum is no longer there. This person I am currently caring for does not even know me. She has no feelings for me. She does not even show any gratitude to what I do for her. For example at some sad moments, I look at this stranger and think, my actual mum would have suffocated me with praise for whatever I am doing for her. My mum would have been calling me with all little loving petty names in praise. She would have been so proud of me. This new mum does not appreciate any services rendered by me and probably takes things for granted. Who wants to be on a "beck and call service" to a person who never says "thank you nor sorry?"

Coming back to my early morning wake up call, after giving mum the requested cold water, I leave her room disgruntled and disappointed for not getting any apology for disturbing my sleep. I get back to bed but cannot fall asleep I remind myself of Barbra Hansen's writings on overcoming sleeplessness. Hansen talks about reaching into the memory bank of mind and cashing in some deposits by letting the words of comfort and inspiration soothe the soul. Most people use simple methods such as silently reminiscing poems, psalms or scriptures which may bring calming effects on their soul and mind. I usually resort to Herbert Benson's relaxation exercises which I learnt at a Women's Religious Group. I work my way through all the muscles of my body which calms my mind as well as my body. One cardinal rule to sleeplessness (never stay in bed wide eyed, as doing so invites dreadful nagging thoughts which keep floating on mind).

However, on this morning, I have gone through all my usual remedies, and before I even count up to sixty, I give up, jump out of bed and head to the kitchen. I make myself a cup of tea and return back to the bedroom with my mind already made up. It is work as usual. I pull out my laptop then I decide to listen to BBC World News before I get carried away with my typing. Ooh dear! There is an earth quake in Turkey. Then Greece needs to be bailed out again and requires another big loan from European Union. I am thinking why is it that most often NEWS is made up of bad or sad stories? Is there nothing Good happening in the world? All right then, I do not want to be depressed any further so I switch off the radio and put on the music while I type away on my laptop.

At 7.35 I jump out of bed after realising I have not given mum her 7 a.m. cup of tea. I am puzzled that mum has not called out for me again since I left her room around 5.30 a.m. I start flattering myself that mum has gotten back to her senses and had realised that she disturbed my sleep therefore she is sorry and has behaved herself. Or is this the wishful thinking I associate with my real mother? For sure, this shadow mother I am caring for must have just fallen asleep herself otherwise she would have called out for me if she was awake.

After serving mum her morning tea, I tell mum we need to have our baths early as I intend to go into town to meet guys with a compressor and drilling machines which are needed for work at the farm. Mum takes no notice of what I am saying, she opens her eyes and turns in her sleep and says, are you going to leave me alone? I say no mum I won't leave you alone I have asked my niece or one of your grandchildren to come and stay with you while I am away. I also add that Katongo (my male house worker) will also be around. Mum goes, ooh no, that Katongo refused to come to my room to bring me water yesterday when you were out. I sit down on mum's bed and say, mum, Katongo has other things to do and sometimes you seem to call out for people when they are busy. Katongo is very good to you and would not refuse to give you water if he knew you wanted any. Mum goes "Eeeh, ulamupela sana insambu nangu nalufyanya" (You always side with him even if he is wrong) I say mum, listen I did not employ Katongo to care for you. He is here to attend to house chores and gardening. After realising this small talk won't take us anywhere, I give up and decide to prepare mum's bath instead.

After finishing with mum, I run myself a bath around 8.30 a.m. I am just about to get in the bath tub when my mobile phone starts ringing. I pick up the phone but can't recognise the number. I recognise the voice at the other end and my blood veins start boiling. The voice goes, "Mwashibukeni, bushe namibusha". "Good morning, did I wake you up?" Inside my heart I am going, blood hell, how dare you think I live in luxury to wake up at 8.30 a.m. don't you realise your mother woke me up at 5.20 a.m. Outwardly, I put on my usual charm and go "Hi, Good morning, no, you did not wake me up. In fact I'm just getting into the bath tub".

The voice goes, "ooh! Sorry, yesterday I could not come to visit mum because I went to the plot, and the carpenter's wife was not well so he did not turn up to meet me there . . . ." I am thinking and what's that got to do with mum. If for instance the carpenter did not report for work then you should have had ample time to visit mum. I thought, let me get into my bath rather than listening to this person's lame excuses for not visiting her mother.

The voice goes, "ooh, aaa, are you there" I answer back and say, yes I am listening. But really I was soaking my embittered body into this warm, foam filled bath and humming away my favourite inspirational song (I will survive . . . .) by Gene Gaynor. I start thinking of how caring my mum was to us. How can I neglect such a wonderful mother at her time of need. Mum needs us and I am answering her call. That is why I have resolved to looking after her irrespective of other siblings' uncaring attitudes.

"Ooh, and the vehicles are not working, the spare parts . . . ." the voice goes on. I am thinking, is she still on the line? "Ooh I must let you have your bath I will call again to check on mum" I am smiling to myself and thinking, I am already in my bath mate! Outwardly I pleasantly say, ooh sorry, I am just adjusting my head cap, ok, then, bye.

I put my phone down. I am still fuming, and I am cursing her. I know I love my sister dearly but I am angry because of what she is doing to mum. Mum has been anxious and confused since her youngest daughter arrived in town a couple of days ago. She sneaks in to visit mum (when I am out) for less than one hour. She tells mum she is not well and has to go and buy eye medicine. As indicated earlier, mum becomes anxious and agitated. When I return home, I find myself being asked questions about my sister's condition. In mum's distorted mind, she does not know I have not even seen my sister nor discussed her eye sore. I am thinking, why did my sister come? She should have just telephoned or something. Mum won't stop worrying about her beloved youngest daughter's eye sore. I foresaw a night of discontent.

After calming mum down and reassuring her that her daughter's eye has improved (I had to tell some white lies) I started reflecting on sacrifices mum had endeavoured in bringing us up. My father was there as well, a nonsense disciplinarian who made everybody know he was head of the house. I loved my dad and I greatly miss him now, but mine was love/fear relationship (don't take me wrong it was not love/hate relationship) We were all petrified of dad mother included but mum took on more when it came to protecting children. She sometimes got a beating from dad if any of us misbehaved at school.

As in other families, dad wanted to discipline the culprit and probably mum interferes and she ends up with a slap on her face. After all it was mum's fault that her child misbehaved at school. Dad's child was the one who came top of class in school exams. My dad was a self-taught ambitious man whose presence could not be missed at any gathering. It is unfortunate that my father was a six footer otherwise I would have used the Bemba saying of (Akalume kepi munshitina mabumba) Dad was fearless and extremely intelligent.

With hind sight Mum had it hard, but that was life in their Victorian era and poor dad was just carrying out his patriarchal duties of the day. Who can blame him? Otherwise he would have just sat there bringing up a bunch of dull uneducated children. How could I have achieved all this knowledge and even have the ability to write about mum's condition. I whole-heartedly attribute all my achievements to dad's dedication and sacrifices. My father sent me to boarding schools despite my parents' meagre financial status at the time. My father installed the competitive nature in me and the desire to do better and he encouraged me to score the highest marks in class. Well done dad! May Your Soul Rest In Peace. I will always be indebted to your visionary aspirations. In return, I will stay put and WAKE UP AT ODD HOURS TO CARE FOR MUMMY I ONLY WISH I COULD DO THE SAME FOR DAD!!!

THE CURSE OF THE
PAWPAW FRUIT

I AM SCRATCHING MY HEAD to develop a healthier diet for mum without upsetting her. Mum for example prefers do noughts to any type of bread. She rarely eats with enthusiasm any type of vegetable. She detects cabbage and many exotic fruits. In her own words, mum tells me a story of a house where she had lived and cabbage was probably the main relish. Oooh, mum says "Twalelya fye ubwali na cilya icimusalu achafumbatana" then mum puts up her hands imitating the shape of cabbage. As for me I collapse laughing. And I jokingly say to mum, so, how are you going to describe the food you are eating at my house? "Eeeh napano pene mumpatikishya ukulya ifyana fya bene" (Yes, even here you force me to eat wild fruits).

I say to mum, look here mum, you have problems with your digestive system and needs to eat a lot of vegetables and fruit and that's why I improvise your diet with a variety of different food stuff as you do not take any vitamin supplements (That was before I started buying B12 and other supplement tablets for her). Sometimes I warn mum against her consistent moaning about her constipation. She usually laments about constipation and how it is going to kill her.

I sometimes try to wine her off her bemoaning mind set and say to her, mum, how come everything seems to be killing you. Mum looks at me in a strange manner then she shrugs her shoulders and moves a bit on the stool she is sitting on and grudgingly says "oooh, you have a younger body and you do not feel any pain" (Awee, kabili uli no bili wa caike tueleuemfwa ubukali nangu bumo) I say to mum that her life is not my kind of life. I tell her I nourish my body by eating sensibly and carry out a few simple exercises. I tell her I am fade up of hearing your mourning about everything and yet you do not seem to like eating sensibly. Mum sulks out loudly and continues accusing me of having a younger body. I get at her and say, look hear mum t here is not a day when you wake up and say you are feeling better. I jokingly say to her, please mum let's have a morning when we greet each other with joy and happiness. I tell her, I am not used to living with somebody who is dying of this pain and that pain every morning.

Mum says things like "Awee, lelo lyena chacilamo filengipaya fye ifi fintu" (Oooh, to day my pains are worse, I am dying of these pains) then I would ask her what exactly is more painful) and mum comes up with a lame answer like "Tefilya fine ndwala" (those things I always suffer from).

Then I may say, mum you need to change your mind set otherwise your illness will never improve and you will definitely die from assumed imaginary diseases. Mum does not like hearing such comments so she could sulk the whole day probably due to the fact that I have mentioned dying to her. My mum is scared of dying. She sometimes says "I am better of dead" (Kuti cawama inga nafwa pantu napesha abantu) but if anybody else talks about dying in old age she gets very upset.

However, the following morning when I take her 7 O'clock morning tea, she tries hard to appear cheerful. She greets me with exaggerated pleasantries and respect. Mum cheerfully says, "Mwashibukeni mukwai" (Good morning madam) I am taken by surprise and I collapse laughing. Having said so and with hind sight, I prefer my mum's false charm as compared to her usual grumbles over her health.

Furthermore, as non-medical person, and in my layman's eyes, I am struggling with thoughts like mum's constipation may be due to taking strong pain killers like paraceutamol, ibuprofen e.t.c. Since I do not give her any vitamin supplements, I have always thought she may benefit and gain nutritious ingredients and minerals by consuming a variety of vegetables and fruits and any foods which are rich in iron and carbohydrates.

On this day in question, I had been out carrying out my weekly shopping. I want to impress mum so I go an extra mile and buy a pawpaw, pears and apples, in addition to her favourite fruits of bananas and oranges. On my arrival I peel the pawpaw fruit and dish out some pieces to her while I also indulge in adding a variety of other fruits to make myself a proper mixed fruit salad. Everything goes well and we retire in our separate bedrooms for a short afternoon rest.

After waking up, I start typing on my laptop then I realise that I should start preparing the evening meal. Mum announces that she does not want to share a baked potatoes with me so I prepare custard porridge mixed with pieces of a peeled banana. Mum loves Custard she can have it any time, morning, lunch or evening. In her own words mum says "Ala nalitutemwa utu utumusunga utwatelela ubusaka" (I love this smooth and tasty porridge).

A few hours later, mum retires to bed. I carry on with my usual typing and decide to go to bed after the ten o'clock news. After an hour or so, I hear the familiar noises of mum's walking stick rattles. I think nothing of it and go back to sleep. But then the noise starts again so I decide to check on mum. I walk slowly in mum's bedroom and find her sitting at the edge of her bed. I inquire if she is okay. She tells me she has a running stomach which is now killing her. I'm thinking, Oh my god there we go with mum's dying business. I say to mum, how many times have you been to the toilet? Mum says many times—and then she says she cannot remember. "Imiku fye iingi teti njibukishe". I say to her, alright then let me fetch you some medicine. I go back into my bedroom and fetch a capsule of Imodium (lop amide) and ask mum to take it with water. I sit with mum until she falls asleep then I go back into my bedroom. Unable to sleep, I pick up a book and start reading, I loose interest almost immediately, I look over and there is what attracts my attention, the laptop. I decide to check on my e mails. Before I know, I am using google to read world News and I get so absorbed. All I hear is the clock alarm going on at 5.30 a.m. I catch my breath and sigh heavily, I start wondering how I will manage with my normal routines during the day when I have hardly had enough sleep. So I decide to switch off everything and lie down in bed.

Little did I know, that mum was awaken by the alarm clock too. The rattle, rattle begins. Mum is hitting the floor with her walking stick in her bedroom—for whatever reason only God knows! I drag myself out off bed and go to mum's room. She hears my footsteps and sits up in bed. She says to me, she has not slept at all "Awe lelo nshishipwilepo fye nangu panono nachesha fye ubushiku bonse" (Ooh, today I haven't slept a wink, I have stayed awake through out the night).

I decide to be diplomatic and inquire tenderly as to what has kept her awake. Then as an after thought I say, it could be the pawpaw fruit which might have been responsible for your running stomach. Mum answers defensively, she says it is your fault I know you always want to poison me by giving me wild fruits. I say half laughing and half seriously to mum, please do not talk of any poisoning business, fruits are good for you. Mum starts accusing me and throws back what I had just said. She goes but you have just told me that eating a pawpaw fruit results in having a running stomach, why are you two faced? (Bushe teiwe walanda ati ukulya pawpaw kulaleta ukupolomya, kanshi ninshi wachenjelala ifi).

I honestly say to mum, listen I am not sure if eating a pawpaw fruit induces diarrhoea but when I lived with my two nieces when I arrived in Zambia they always teased me for my love for pawpaw fruit. Each time I asked them about their dislike of pawpaw fruit they told me that eating pawpaw fruit gives them running tummies. I had a real ball, the pawpaw tree was in fact in our yard and I ate pawpaw fruit night and day to the annoyance of my nieces who threatened not to take me to hospital if I ever complained of any stomachache.

MULENGA

19TH SEPTEMBER, 2011 STARTS LIKE any other day. There is an electric atmosphere of anticipation in the air. I am talking about the election fever, the country has gone ago go. Tomorrow 20th September, 2011 Zambia goes to the polls to choose a new government.

It is a beautiful morning and I have to force myself to wake up. On reflection, I woke up in a cheerful mood after being woken by the melodies from the birds which have made a nest on the gutter of my bedroom window. I stretch myself and jump out of bed, I wrap myself up in a gown and tiptoe to the bathroom. I have to be careful as I hate waking up mum before I brush my teeth nor wash my face.

I walk back in my bedroom and proceed to the kitchen where I hastily switch on the kettle and pour out two mugs of tea. I then proceed to mum's room and cheerfully say, "Good morning mum", (Mwashibukeni ba mayo). Mum gives her popular heavy grunt of "Uugh uugh". I automatically know, things are not great with mum and I prepare and psyche myself for impending laments about her illnesses. I tenderly say to mum, are you okay mum? (Ninshi ba mayo, bushe namulwala lelo). Mum slowly opens her eyes and says, "Nimfwa ine" (I am dead). Half laughing and partially trying to make sense of what mum is talking about I diplomatically say to her "How can you be talking to me if you are dead?" Have you ever heard of a dead person speaking and turning in bed? Mum who is already in a defiant mood opens her eyes and looks at me then she says: "Awee teba Docas banjipaya iyoo, nimbafu bamfuna uko nali eshanjipaya" (It is not SDA Docas who are killing me it is the broken ribs, the injury I sustained when I was tossed in the air that is killing me) Mum has this thing in her head that she was once mishandled when a grandson who is a professional nurse tenderly lifted her and put her to bed on the night she was agitated over something and was refusing to get in bed independently.

Each time I speak to my nephew within mum's earshot and he asks to speak to her, mum coils up in fear and says, "Ooh, ooh, not that one I do not want to talk to him because he tossed me in the air and then threw me on bed (Awee teti nande nao, ulya uwamposele mumulu elyo amponya pa beti). To please mum I could exaggerate a little and purposely and loudly say to my nephew on the phone, how could you do such a thing to my mother eeh? By then my nephew and myself could be in stitches as he protests and tries between fits of laughter to explain to me exactly what happened. After all it was him who was sponsoring mum's upkeep whilst she was living with his mother (my elder sister) on the copper belt and I am satisfied that there is no way my nephew who is a trained male nurse could have tossed mum in the air and then drop her on bed, fragile as she is.

For all I know, mum experiences hallucinations and sometimes delusions which she perceives as real incidents. In her confusion, she picks on different people and makes wild allegations against them. As far as she is concerned those allegations are real incidents which stick in her distorted mind.

Another allegation is that while I was away on my Christmas break my niece who spent a few days caring for mum at my house made a comment on mum's blouse. My niece jokingly said "Grandma this is a nice top, I am sure it can look nicer on me as I am a younger person". (Awee mama aka akashati mufwele kasuma kalingile fye ine nemukashana ukufwala) Mum did not answer her back but was furious and came up with a weird story a few weeks later.

However on my return back home mum started insinuating that my niece had stolen all her clothes. On inspection all mum's clothes were still intact in her wardrobe. When I confronted mum about sincerity and explained to her that as an SDA Christian she should not be making false allegations against family members who are actually caring for her. Mum turned nasty and told me that I am also another person who has stolen her money. I was shocked at mum's utterances, naturally I sat her down and gave her a good telling off. A few months later, mum starts preaching to anybody who visits us at home that on her arrival at my house from the Copper Belt, she had enough money for her own burial but that the owner of the house and her workers have stolen all of it. In her own words she says "Kabili abene ba ng'anda naba nchito bakwe eba njibila shyonse impiya naishile nashyo ishyakunshikilamo".

However, the first time I heard her telling people this story I was devastated and embarrassed. I wondered as to what kind of money mum came with from the Copperbelt when I am in fact the person who financed her passage. I had arranged for my niece to fetch her and paid for both fares which included a little pocket money for both of them. How much money did she have on her on her arrival which was enough for her burial? I often remind mum that the money she gives as weekly offering to her SDA Church eats into her little savings. Probably mum thinks each time she makes an offering to Church, God sends it back to her.

Sometimes, it amuses me when mum after counting her monies with Anne (her assistant and trustee) finds out that her budget is dwindling down and starts sulking. She sometimes says "Eeeh, impiya shandi nashipwa, shileonaka fye kabili shilya mpela ubupe ku church nashyo tashibwela iyoo". (All my money is finished even the money I give as offering to church never comes back). On such occasions and depending on her prevailing mood, I usually poke jokes at her that God won't accept her church offering if she continuously bemoans about it.

Poor mum, what can she do, her budget consists of little hand outs from family especially grand children. There is no social security nor state pension as of now in Zambia. The elderly and unemployed have to fend for themselves. It is a dire situation. The difference between the deserving and undeserving is as wide as the Atlantic Ocean. It is unbearable and it is a phenomenal which breaks my heart. Sometimes I wake up in the middle of night and pray to God that something is done about it. It is a situation which THINK TANKS need to address. On mum's good day, I would joke and tease her that mum you are so thrifty, what would happen if you earned your money by working under stressful and stringent conditions. Mum would reply and say, whatever my children have achieved and accumulated is mine. "Fyonse ifyabombela abana bandi, fyandi, kabili nine Mulenga, walenga fyonse. Ukwabula ine inga teti mukwate fyonse ifi ifyuma". (All what my children have worked for is mine, after all, none of you would have been able to accumulate all possessions without me, I am the creator or instigator) Rather amused, I exclaim at her and say, but what did you give to your parents mum? How can we (children) surrender everything we own to you? What are we leaving for our own children? Mum would just ignore my utterances and carry on claiming my possessions and those of my siblings to be hers. Then I would tease her and say, how about dad, hasn't he got a share to claim? In my heart I am praying and saying leave my father alone, after all he is the one who laboured to find money for our school fees and yet he never lived long enough to reap what he sow (MHSRIP). Mum would just look at me and give her disapproving grunt of "uuugh".

Coming back to our morning tea, mum grudgingly agrees to sit up and accepts a mug of tea while I sit on the stool next to her bed sipping mine. I wait quietly for another pronouncement. Mum glances at her mug which I had placed on a saucer. She touches the handle of the mug and shakes it. This practice is meant to ensure that there is a saucer under the mug. Never give mum a cup of tea or mug without a saucer she will refuse to drink it. One wonders where mum got these middle class manners. Having spent most of her life in a semi rural environment, before she eventually moved into Mansa, a small town North-East Zambia one expects mum to be more of a passive, domant person with no special preferences. Eeeh! not with mum, she sometimes puts on so much airs and I have to tell her to tone down.

Eventually, mum drinks her tea in silence and afterwards, I take back the two mugs to the kitchen. I then proceed to prepare mum's bath and coax her to come to the bath room. Before she even says it, I know what mum is going to say, it is either the water is too cold or too hot. In her own words she says "Amenshi yatalala, or yakabishya" I usually ask mum in my dire frustration things like "When on earth are you going to say something which will please your carer? Haven't you got any good words in your vocabulary and where is your diplomacy? (Bushe imwe mayo tamulandapo ifintu ifisuma nangu tamwaishiba ukutasha uulemisunga? Sometimes mum answers back and says "Yes one day I will die from being scolded. I am forever suffering". (Ine nkafwa fye kufyebo elyo nkafwa ndecula) I just look at mum and feel sorry for her. Deep down my heart I am thinking that true to God the mother I know would not say anything like that, you are a stranger who is trapped in my mother's body.

Feeling empty and dejected, I assist mum get in the bath and assist with drying up. I choose clothes for her, which also becomes another battle field. She either does not like the black one or the multi coloured one nor chitenge garment until she makes up her mind of what she wants to wear. If I inquire why she is becoming so difficult she answers back and says "Eeeh, pantu lyonse ulempatikisha ukufwala efyo nshilefwaya" (Eeeh, because you are always forcing me to wear what I do not like) Sometimes I swallow hard and think, this is not what I thought looking after mum would lead to. I regret having put myself in such a situation while I would have happily been leading a different life altogether. Why do I have to fight with this shell of a mother, where is this leading me to? Do other siblings know what I am going through, I quietly sob.

However, I quickly prepare breakfast for mum as I have in mind the thought of popping into town to top up on our rations as nobody knows what tomorrow 20th September will be like with all the election fever oozing around the country. Little did I know that the day would pass graciously and peacefully especially in the part of town where I live the only noises I heard were of barking dogs who were alarmed by fireworks' noises coming from a far away field.

I say to mum, I need to hurry up and get myself sorted out before I quickly pop into town. Mum goes, where do you always go? You like leaving me alone. I want you to stay with me at home. I turn round and say, mum I am on my own and I have to provide for both of us so I have to go out and source funds for us to buy food and all house essentials. Mum goes but you always go out, what do you do there? "Finshi mucita uko muya?" I try to explain to mum, that I sometimes attend meetings. Mum goes what are meetings for and what do you always litigate about? (Finshi mulubulula lyonse?) I answer back and say "Awe tatulubulula tulanda ifya kucita mumibombele yesu. I say to mum, listen mum I am running late I need to have a bath and dash off to town. Mum looks at me and says "Awee shifwaya ukuti iwe wafumapo, ndeumfwa icitendwe" (I do not want you to go away because I feel lonely). I say but there are other people who remain with you mum. As I utter those words, I feel a lump in my throat. I feel for mum who is desperately lonely and isolated hence she needs my company at all times. Where can I take her? There is no Day Care Centre for the elderly nor a recreational centre where people of my mother's age could be dropped by working relatives and be picked up later in the evenings. I just feel resentful and I do not know what to do. I quickly run the bath and soak my aching bones.

Incidentally, as I sit in the bath tub, a thought quickly passes through my brains. I am thinking, I do not like this caring role. I do not like the fact that mum has been abandoned on me by other siblings shamelessly. I am thinking, should I go back to England or stay and live with this stranger? For how long am I going to put up with this unpaid frustrating role? In those few seconds, I just felt so helpless and hopeless. Most of all, I felt resentful to both mum and my siblings.

Then I start thinking of all my projects in making and I say loudly, I am staying, but on condition that I write about my experiences. I think cheerfully to myself that mum is going to be the main character in my book and I will endeavour to observe all her movements, activities, utterances bad and good moods and see what I will come up with. From that moment, I could not wait to be near mum so that I could hear and write down what she says or does. I even welcomed telephone calls from my siblings which were as usual full of lame excuses, they all became part of the story. This is how I started jotting down mum's perception of her world, her utterances, fears, bad and good moods and indeed my own feelings which have informed this book. My book was thought about in a bath tub after months of dire frustration.

It goes without saying that "Nothing is more powerful than a thought-through idea" I must confess that the idea of writing a book which dawned on me in a bath tub has saved me from moments of sheer frustration and despair.

In my heart of hearts though, I have other people who may be going through the same experiences of having to care for elderly relatives who suffer from old age dementia and having nowhere to get help from. Couldn't it be nice to have a forum of careers on Zambian Television debating on issues relating to caring roles just as there are forums for traditional marriage counselling (bana cimbusa) e.t.c. Why should debates on dementia or any disease affecting the elderly be regarded as "taboo?"

My remote hope and vision is that somebody in an influential position reads my book and probably urges our government to take into consideration the plight of elderly people in Zambian communities. The elderly people are just as vulnerable as people with disabilities, homeless children (street kids) and any other grouping looming on the fledges of our society. After all they are our fathers and mothers who laboured for us why should we, their children forsake them? Let our government introduce projects on Dementia Awareness in our communities. Remember, these very people, fragile and confused as they are today, made sacrifices for you and me.

Don't you think they deserve to end their final journey gracefully and die with respect and dignity which is rightly due to them?

HAVE YOU TELEPHONED
THE PRESIDENT?

IT IS PASSED MIDNIGHT AND I am fast asleep. I wake up with a start after hearing loud screams. I sit up in bed and rub my eyes. Am I dreaming? Am I the one shouting? Within seconds, I hear the commotion, mum is hitting her walking stick on the floor, on the door and walls then I hear a loud scream—Oowee! Mutulee eeeh! Nafwaa inee! (Help! I am dying, somebody help me!).

I jump out off bed and run towards mum's bedroom. I am thinking, is mum fainting or fitting. For all I know people who faint or fit do not make such a commotion neither do they scream. I bump into mum in the door way. She is tilting her head forwards and backwards and at the same time calling for help. I get hold of her, I grab the walking stick from her. I start shaking her and at the same time asking her as to what is happening to her. I call out to her, what the hell is going on here? Are you fitting or what? Mum is still hysterical and is fighting me off. She is trying to get off my grip. I sense that immediately I let go off her, she is going to fall down and hurt her self at the same time a small professional voice is telling me not to break her fall nor allow myself to fall down with her as I will be the one who will be hurt.

I am now divided between letting her fall down or lift her and place her on bed. On my first try to lift her, I fail. I am thinking God, mum is heavy, what do I do next? Should I let her fall down then drag her along to bed. This option is too cruel to pursue then I start imagining myself applying First Aid to mum. First I check to ensure that she is breathing, which she is; next I think of stabilizing her fall which is what I am doing. Thirdly I think of handling and lifting techniques. As though on camera, I quickly swing left and hold mum from behind placing my hands firmly under her armpits. I count up to five and summon all the strength in my body then pull mum backwards. We both go flying on her bed. I breathe a sigh of relief at least it has worked and my effort has paid off.

I place mum in a recovery position. I check her air passage then rush to the bath room. I pull a large bathing towel, soak it in cold water and then I run back in mum's bedroom and place the dampened towel over her head. Mum is sweating profusely and is still calling out for help.

A few minutes later, mum calms down and stops shouting. I wipe her face with the damp towel coax her to lie still for a few minutes. I rush in my bedroom and pick up the phone and start calling for assistance. I am not sure whether mum needs medical attention but I need someone to give their opinion as well. I first telephone my brother who lives on the other side of town, he responds almost immediately and promises to drive down as soon as possible. Then I remember that my friend Abbia lives only five minutes away from me in the same neighbourhood. I also put a call through to her. She assures me that she will be coming as soon as possible. Then I ring my sister just to let her know that mum is not well. The call goes un answered. I go back to check on mum whom I find in a sitting position despite the fact that I had asked her to lie down without moving. I ask mum how she is feeling and avoid telling her off. Mum ignores my questioning looks at me and says, what were you doing in your bedroom? I answer her and say, I was making telephone calls. Mum asks, whom were you telephoning? I say to her, I was telephoning my brother and my friend Abbiah. Mum looks at me and says, have you telephoned the President? "Bushe nautuminina ba Kateka?" I am alarmed and tickled. I say to mum, which President are you referring to? Mum answers and says the one who was elected last week. "Inga aba basalile uyu mulungu wafumineko". I am amazed at mum's accuracy and I want to prolong our small chat before she changes the subject. I look at mum who is speaking so calmly and natural and I say to her, I am thinking, is this the same person who was screaming her head off. In just a short time she is so sensible and is naming presidents. To hide my sudden amazement I ask mum and say how do you know there is a new president? Do you know his name? Mum says I know, is it not Mr Saka? "Ninjishiba, bushe tali Saka?" I burst out laughing, I say well done mum, you are almost right the president's name is Sata and not Saka. How do you know about presidents? Unperturbed and appearing more confident mum adjusts her position and says the only president

I liked is Kaunda (Referring to the 1ˢᵗ Republican President of Zambia Dr. Kenneth Kaunda) In her own words she says "Kateka natemenwe ni Kaunda". I am now holding my breath and in an encouraging voice I say to mum, why did you like president Kaunda? Mum goes because he was telling people wise things. "Kaunda alelanda ifyamano". I say to mum, please mum hold on a second let me go and prepare you a warm drink then you will tell me all about wise advice Kaunda gave to his people.

I quickly run out of mum's room and start warming up milk for her. In the next second, I hear a big knock on the door. I am thinking oh no, they are going to spoil it all, (I am referring to the people I rang earlier) I am thinking mum won't tell me about Kaunda in the presence of other people. If anything she will come up with another mysterious illness which will frighten all of us. Anyway I hide my disappointment and go to answer the door. Actually both my brother and Abbia and her husband arrive almost at the same time. They look at my face, probably trying to detect the seriousness of mum's illness but I am laughing and at the same time ushering them inside the house. Abbia and my brother rush to mum's bedroom while I lead her husband to sit on my bed (remember, those are the days before my household goods arrived. I then join Abbia and my brother in mum's bedroom. They are both looking at mum then they look at me. I burst out laughing. To please mum, I purposely say to them, mum was very ill, however, has recovered so well it is unbelievable, she is now telling me stories about Zambian presidents, both Abbia, her husband and my brother look at me with puzzled stares. I then go and sit on mum's bed with my mug of hot milk in my hand and say, mum can you tell us something about president Kaunda, mum goes "aada"! I say mum please do not be like that we were having a nice chat about president Kaunda, now you are pretending you do not know what I am talking about. Mum goes "Awee ndefwaya ukulala" (I want to sleep) I say to mum drink your warm milk and we will leave you to go to sleep. Then we retreat in my bedroom and we start laughing. I start by apologizing for waking them up in the middle of the night. At the same I assure them that mum presented crazy symptoms of her illness. I tell them I felt frightened and that is why I called for assistance. Anyway they accept my apology and we ended the night by appreciating mum's intelligence and wondered how she ear dropped about the new president being sworn in.

MY TEARS FOR MUMMY

IT IS A MONDAY MORNING. It's the sixth day since my baby sister arrived in town from her home on the Copperbelt. My sister did not visit mum over the weekend. Mum is anxiously asking when her daughter is visiting her. I have a couple of things I want to attend to in town. I cannot leave mum alone and I am reluctant to ask my niece to come and care for mum in my absence (this is before I normalised the situation and started paying for my niece's services). I am thinking I asked my niece yesterday, Sunday to come and help me out since I had an urgent errand to attend to, hence I am not keen to make another request. I make up my mind and decide to ask my male worker to look after mum while I quickly pop out in town.

I know mum loves Katongo although she sometimes mourns that Katongo leaves her alone and spends most time at his house (servant quarters) when I am away. However, deep down my heart I know why Katongo takes time to go to his rooms. He needs a break from mum's constant interrogation. Mum says to me "Bushe Katongo ninshi acita mu ng'anda yakwe inga wafumapo?" What does Katongo do in his house when you are away? I answer mum and say, I do not know but I will talk to him about it. Mum goes, "Bushe ukamulipila impiya uno mweshi? Awe akashitola fye". Are you paying him this month? That will be money he has not worked for! I just feel blood rising in my veins but I control myself and just leave mum to her devices while I busy myself with something else. I am at the same time thinking what can I do without the understanding of Katongo who agrees at any time to look after mum. How can I not pay him his wages for taking a break from his added caring role? And funny enough mum would start praising Katongo within minutes of discrediting him. I basically attribute mum's temperamental fluctuations of character to her difficult behaviours brought on by old age dementia. In order to amuse myself and happily focus on other things, I recite the analogy which says "When the cat is away, the mouse goes loose". So, Katongo is not committing a crime by frequenting his dwellings in my absence.

However, coming back to my trip into town, I walk to the bus stop and catch a mini bus. I meet up with my clients then decide to do a mini grocery shopping which starts with a pound of apples and by the time I finish going round the shop's alleys, the trolley is full and I come out of the shop with six carrier bags.

I am smiling to myself as I stand outside the supermarket for I already know the kind of language I'll endure from the mini bus conductor for getting on his bus with so many bags. I am debating whether I should call a taxi. But then I am thinking I will just pay a fraction of a taxi fare if I get on the mini bus as long as I am brave enough to stand the conductors' flowery language. Oh, I sometimes laugh at the way conductors phrase their comments in Bemba or Nyanja. For example, I was once waiting for a mini bus on Great East Road after dispatching my driver to an urgent errand on the other side of town. Two mini buses came racing from Chelstone. The first one scared the hell out of me as it's brakes made such screeching noises on it's emergency stopping, even other waiting passengers ran away. Anyway I followed other passengers to the second mini bus and ignored the conductor of the first bus who was blocking my way and gauging me to get into his mini bus. The ignored conductor looked at me from head to toe then he said "Imwe a mai oina sembe namipasa full seat pa bus yanga" (Hey lady, you are a fat woman, I should have given you a full seat on my bus) I did not answer back but quietly I am cursing him, I am mouthing out things like, how dare you say such insulting things to me. I jump on the second bus with the approval of it's conductor who now starts boasting about the nice perfume he had smelt on me. He goes to other passenger, "Eeeh ladies! Leave enough space for this nice smelling lady" (Imwe bana mayo seleleni uko, lekeni abalenunka perfume bekale bwino). I just burst out laughing. I am thinking, within a couple of minutes I have both been insulted and now I am receiving over-board compliments. I happily thought to myself "welcome to Zambian mini bus service".

Moreover, I urge myself to concentrate and focus on the trip ahead of me, so I psyche myself and pull up all six shopping bags plus my hand bag towards Makeni Kankole bus stop. I am thinking, okay, I will be very nice to the conductor and ask to pay for two seats so that I can have enough space for my shopping bags and self without ever being scolded for having a big bum and carrying six shopping bags on his bus.

There comes the conductor enticing me half way calling out "Makeni Kankole, Makeni Kankole mwashala" "Eeeeh Ma-ke-ni Ka-nko-le t-w-o" And that's exactly what I want to hear, the calling is so dramatised and at the same time aromatised and one feels welcomed in an unfamiliar way. To put it more precisely, the relationship between mini bus conductor and passenger feels like holding a broken glass with rough edges which can hurt at the lightest mishandling so one concentrates on holding it with care. Sweet as conductors appear when enticing you to get on their respective buses, they can turn nasty and swear at you within seconds at any slightest provocation.

To-day I am very lucky. The conductor grabs my bags and ushers me to take the front seat. He looks around calling for passengers and spots a very slim girl coming towards his mini bus he quickly goes and encircles her and leads her to take the front seat with me. Oh, clever conductor, he is my hero and I am praising him for his cunning manevours and I feel really honoured by his quick thinking. Within seconds the bus is full and we are en route to Makeni. Not forgetting the ear-bashing music which everybody is exposed to. I am sitting there praying that nobody rings me whilst on the bus as I could not hear the caller with such deafening melodies blowing away. I thought of the time I visited Milan (Italy) with a friend, people spoke to us in Italian in streets and shops but immediately we boarded a bus or metro, there was loud music by American or British artists. It felt like home and I am thinking this is the beauty of public transport, it blows away ones sorrows and one concentrates on the now while being entertained to music or unprovoked fights.

However, now I am thinking, how do I get home after dropping off at Londola Road with all my shopping bags. I decide to call for help. Then I remind myself that Katongo is caring for mum and would not come to meet me. Bingo! I remember Abbia, my childhood friend who lives five minutes' drive from me. I pull out my phone and whisper into it. I say to Abbia, listen honey, I am on the mini bus but I have six shopping bags with me, could you meet me at Londola Bus Stop and give me a lift home. Abbia says, yes I will wait for you there. The mini bus stops with the usual screeching noises at Londola Road and Abbia is already parked there waiting for me.

We put bags into her car and drive home together. Oh, Abbia my dear friend, when we meet we are just like two little naught girls. We met in Kabwe in 1972 just after completing Form V. We came from different schools. Abbiah from Mufulira (a town girl) and me from Kasama Girls (a village pumpkin). We just hit it off like fire. However, we went separate ways when Form V results came out. I went to Nkwame Nkhruma Teachers College while Abbiah continued and graduated at Kabwe Trades Institute. We both married our childhood sweethearts and met up in Lusaka again where we both settled with our young families. In the late seventies both our husbands were sponsored to study abroad and we both followed our husbands despite our young families. Abbia and her family returned back to Zambia after a couple of years while my family remained in England up to the present day. I met Abbia again in August 2011 after a long spell of time, two weeks after I moved into the Makeni area. This was a blessing because Abbia is my sister in making. I can give Abbia my kidney if it came to that and I am sure she can do like-wise.

However we reached my house after a short drive and both of us are in stitches laughing away at nothing and everything. I sometimes tease Abbia and say, am I your favourite cousin or do you see human spoils on me for you to be laughing at me each time you set eyes on me. Abbia chokes away laughing. Oh dear, Abbia is so funny! I love her to bits. However, on our arrival at my house, Katongo helps unloading bags from Abbia's car and myself and Abbia, still giggling head off to mum's room. As I expected, mum mistakes Abbiah for my little sister when she hears our laughing noises. On our entry, mum is sitting on her bed with this big smile plastered all over her face. There is this big glow of happiness about her.

Before I can even think properly, I look at Abbia and unconsciously say, Abbia, look mum is smiling. We both throw a "knowing" look at each other. But immediately, Abbia opens her mouth to say hello mum how are you? I notice the glow on mum's face fading away while a fixed smile is still there. I take a step forward and say, hello mum, I am back and I am so happy to see you smile, what is it that Katongo gave you for lunch that makes you feel so happy? Mum goes "tapali ifyo ampele" (he gave me nothing). We ate beans and fresh fish and nshima for lunch. I said coaxingly, ooh, mum I know as a Luapula woman, you love fish and I am sure you had a good meal. Mum goes "awee nacilya fye cilemba nakabwali aka nono" (I only ate beans with a little piece of nshima) I am thinking there we go, this new mother I live with is never grateful she twists everything from positive to negative. So I drop the subject and after Abbia manages to extract a small chat with her, we leave mum's room for the kitchen and finally Abbia announces she has to get back home soonest as she has to pick up grand children from school.

So, I decide to see Abbia off and I walk with her to the car. Out of the blue I start confiding in her by saying, Abbia, mum mistook you for her baby daughter that's why she sat up on her bed with that big smile plastered all over her face. Abbia stops walking and looks at me. This time she is not laughing and I could see fiery in her eyes. Abbia calmly says "but your sister should be helping you care for your mother especially when she is in town she should visit your mother more frequently or take her out somewhere to give you a break". I did not answer Abbia back. I felt a lump in my throat. I wave to her as she drives away and rushes back into the house.

I go straight into my bedroom and throw myself on bed. I start weeping. I cry for mum's undying love for her baby daughter which goes un reciprocated. I am thinking, does my sister realise how painful it is to love somebody who does not show any love for you? I repeated to myself mum is too demented to realise that her youngest daughter is a grown up individual with her own family and has other loves in her life. In short, she has moved on and loved other people.

I cry for my longing for freedom which I now do not have. I cry for my previous funny-loving mother whom I feel I have lost. I cry for my children and grandchildren whom I have left motherless in England. I keep asking myself as to who is cooking Sunday dinners for my children? Who is spoiling my grandchildren when I am not there? Who is taking my grandchildren to Sunday school? Have I done the right thing to leave the life I know, the people I treasure and the familiar environment I can walk blind-folded in to come to my mother country where people are so hard and un compromising? Why did I come anyway, after all these years? And who is this difficult stranger they have abandoned on me? Where are other siblings? Do they realise mum needs them more now than ever before? Where is my social life? I cry and cry!!

Then I hear a knock on my door! Madam, madam, knock, knock, I say "yes" I wouldn't dare say "come in" as I know that I am in a terrible state. Katongo says, madam your phone is ringing. I say to him, I am coming, thank you. I get up off bed, and walk into my en suite bathroom and splash cold water all over my face. I pull the towel and dry my face then I walk to the kitchen where I had left my phone.

I see a missed call with a London code I do not recognise the number. I dial back with my heart in my mouth I am thinking, who is this person, what has happened? Then, there comes a familiar voice at the other end of the phone saying "Eeeh, iwee, Chama" the voice goes. I swallow hard and smile—oh dear, it is ba Magdalene Chibangu one of my favourite Luapula cliques in London. She goes, iwee, Grace, listen I am dancing to Spokes Chola's song, can you hear it. I burst out laughing. I am saying to her, ba Magdalene please give me a break, how can you dance to Spokes Chola's song in the middle of the day are you having a Zambian party at your house? She goes, no, no, there is no party ndekufuluka fye (I am longing for you) so I thought I should play the "King's music. Me and ba Magdalene refer to Spokes Chola as our Elvis Presely. So we have nick-named him the Luapula King of Music. On any happy occasion, myself and ba Magdalene could be there listening and dancing to Spokes Chola songs till late.

I say to myself, this is the kind of life I am missing—talking and mixing with people who are so simultaneous. People you can laugh with! Discuss business with or simply go out to "chill up" with. Oh poor me! I am stuck with a shadow of a mother who is ravaged by the on-set of dementia. I feel the lump threatening to block my throat again but I firmly tell myself NO MORE CRYING YOU ARE ON THE PHONE. Ba Magdalene is going on "Chama, how is Zambia?" Ba Magdelene has never been to Zambia since the collapse of Zambia Airways. She amuses me when she tells me as Zambia Airways employee, she was on the last Zambia Airways flight to London and never returned back home despite the fact that other passengers were relocated to Air Mozambique. So ba Magdelene has this spiritual hyped romanticized picture of Zambia. I therefore take advantage of her ignorance and pull her socks by magnifying every aspect of new buildings, social and economic growth in Zambia to her. So in response, I say to her, Zambia is amazing, it is fantastic, it is fabulous and beautiful". Deep down my heart I am saying "It is a rough, hard and crucifying life out here hence I am in tears while talking to you". However, to disguise my misery and untold longing and to avoid crying out loud, I outwardly and pleasantly say, Oh ba Magdalene, I have run out of talk time, my credit is finishing on the phone, bye. She says I will call you later at night, waumfwa Chama! I say to her, Eee, eee mukwai, and thanks for calling! good bye! I throw the phone on my bed.

Then, tears start pouring out of my eyes like rain A-G-A-I-N.

UNDER SIEGE

IT IS A SUNDAY MORNING, and I know I am on my own. I have no domestic help as Mr Katongo has insisted that he is a staunch Born Again Christian and never misses a Sunday service. Well, who am I to stop anybody from carrying out such a noble activity.

However, I am sceptical of Mr Katongo's religious endeavours as it is only on Sunday evenings that I see him coming back home to his servants' quarters walking in such a manner which appears like a cross between walking on fire or crossing a muddy river. His speech, if anyone has courage to listen to him is slurred and gambled and his eyes are bloody red. Probably all these characteristics are due to the singing and chanting at his church.

Incidentally, the other Sunday evening he came back home clutching his hands on his head. When I inquired I was told that a rude child threw a stone at him. I may not be a doctor nor a nurse, but a stone injury leaves an open wound, bruise or cut while a fist blow leaves a bump isn't it? There was a small swelling on the side of his head.

Having said so, myself and Mr Katongo have come to an agreement that Sunday is his day off and whatever he does with his free time is his business as long as he reports on duty sober on Monday morning that's fine with me.

I start my day by watering my newly dug garden. Remember I moved houses and I have left my well developed garden at Flat 2. For the one and half months I lived at Flat2 I managed to grow a variety of vegetables which I am still harvesting and eating—of course with the permission of the current occupier. My new garden is bigger and I have even ventured into sowing exotic vegetables/plants like beetroot, egg plant, tomatoes, onions, cassava leaf, Irish potatoes, pumpkin leaf, sage or (five years leaf) okra e.t.c. I am quite pleased with my new garden.

My next activity is to make mum her 7 a.m. cup of tea then washing up dishes and tidying up the kitchen and the sitting room. On this morning like any other Sunday mornings I try to take two mugs of tea so that I can sit with mum for a few minutes while we drink our morning tea. I try to explain to her that we have no help and that the two of us will have to help each other wherever necessary. On good days mum would say "cinshi mulefwaya incite?" (what do you want me to help you with? Or what can I do?) Otherwise mum cannot comprehend why Katongo nor Ann are not on duty. Mum would come up with a list of things they did wrong the previous day. I just have to agree with mum and stir her away from such a subject.

On this morning, mum's door is closed which is rare I try to leave her door slightly ajar after putting her to bed every night. I knock on mum's door and mum does not respond at all. I am holding two mugs of tea and my heart hastens and I am thinking of all bad reasons why mum's door is closed and why mum can't respond to my knock. I think of putting one mug down and have a free hand. Unfortunately, my adeline kicks in and before I know, I am kicking the door down. I burst in the room, I am shell shocked for there is mum cowering on her bed in a foetal position clinging to a key which she is firmly holding in her right hand.

I yell out to mum with both mugs still in my hands. I shout out at her. I am both asking and accusing her. I quickly, say mum, are you alright? (Ba mayo, cinshi?) Mum looks up, still scared and trembling. Mum says, we are under siege, haven't you seen them? They have come to pick us up. "Ala natusanswa, bushe taubamwene, nabesa mukutwikata ". I breathlessly ask mum more than one question. I am almost shouting at her. I say, whom are you referring to and why have you got that key in your hand? "Bakapokola bacilafwaya ukunyingilila elyo nabutuka naisala icibi" (the police wanted to enter my room but I quickly ran to the door and locked it) Ooh! My god! Where is the police and besides your bedroom door was just closed and not locked. "Inga ba police bali kwi? Elyo icibi cachiba icha isalwa tamwa cikomako iyoo". Mum becomes defensive and says "Eee eee naiwe wine tawacilafwaya ukwisa ngiswilako, nacilakwita wacikana ukwisa ngiswila". (It is your fault, I was calling out for you and you refused to come and unlock the door for me). I say to mum, listen, nobody tried to enter your room and I have always warned you against running to the door as you may fall down. And besides if you lock yourself up in this room, you will not be able to unlock the door from inside.

Mum sits up and says, I saw police passing by my window and I heard them enter the house. "Nacibamona bakapokola balepita pa window elyo baingila mu ng'anda". I tell mum in a very calm voice that it is me who was watering the garden outside and I came back inside the house to boil the kettle to make morning tea for us. Mum hardly listens to what I am saying. In response she says "Nacibamona bakapokola ba cibalo". Then, I breathe out air of relief. I realise then that mum is back to the 40s/50s where colonial police went round workers' houses, arresting the unemployed or people without identity passes (icitupa). I am telling myself, think, quickly and take your mum out of this mode. I scratch my head and I decide that the best thing is to talk about this elizabethian era with mum. So I sit down on mum's bed and hand her a mug of tea.

I say to mum, okay mum, let us talk about these colonial police who terrorised people in their houses. (cisuma mayo nshimikileniko ifyalecitika ilyo bakapokola ba chibalo baleisa muma yanda yenu). Mum sips tea from her mug and focus ahead of her then she goes "uuugh uugh". Then mum answers me and says "nindaba, nshileibukisha nangu cimo". (I have forgotten, I can't remember anything). Secretly, I am pleased that mum is at least responding to me and I know she is thinking about something else and is no longer frightened.

I am trying hard to analyse mum's fears stemming from events which happened such a long time ago. Then I remember a disturbing episode told to me by a colleague, who did part time work as a residential social worker in Residential and Nursing Homes around London. She said one weekend she was working as Officer in-charge at a 64 bed residential home in Essex. This was at the start of the First Gulf War (the one started by George Bush snr and Margaret Thatcher in 1991). She said all television channels were bellowing the bombings of Bagdad. She said the more reports on Bagdad bombings rained down on television channels the more some residents became anxious and visibly upset.

My colleague further confided in me that being of African origins, she could not make sense of what was happening until one white elderly officer explained to her that the bombings on television is reminiscence of bombing raids on London which took place during the Second World War (commonly referred to as the London Blitz) which mostly affected the East End of London where most of the residents at that Essex Home originated from. It appeared, that some residents at this Home had personally experienced the London Blitz hence they suffered flash backs at the sight of Bagdad Bombings.

My colleague said, in order for her to restore peace and order in the Home, she had no choice but to instruct care assistants to change channels on all television sets or switch off the television sets all together and engage residents in other activities such as playing cards or playing bingo or merely playing music in residents' lounges.

Reciting and comparing the two incidents which took place in two very different environments and societies but had similar impacts on people who underwent similar experiences though in different continents, different cultures and at different times made me realise that symptoms of on set dementia are very similar in all races. It also made me to start approaching mum's illness cautiously and with a lot of compassion.

DEL'S NARROW ESCAPE

MUM, AS EXPLAINED IN PREVIOUS chapters has developed selective hearing, sight and even talking. Mum can stubbornly refuse to speak to anybody and may only speak to people she feels like talking to. As though ignoring people is not good enough, mum only sees things she wants to see.

For example she has told everybody including myself that she can not see and that her sight has gotten so bad that she cannot differentiate between day and night. I always remind her that not knowing the difference between day and night has nothing to do with sight but is caused by distortion in ones' brains and is entirely a mental processing mishap. I tell mum that she is not totally blind as she can make out some images and probably see certain things normally. But mum swears over my head (her daughter) that most difficulties she is experiencing is due to her failing eye sight fair enough, however there are incidents when mum sees the least thing you expect her to see—things like paper money, chitenge materials, colour of her slippers e.t.c.

However, one day I questioned mum's degree of her poor sight. This is me coming in the house completely exhausted and with drips of sweat running down my back. I go straight into my bedroom, strip off the pair of jeans, and a soaking t/shirt. I pull out a pair of shorts then I change my mind as mum keeps telling me off for wearing shortened shorts. I then pull out a mini M&S cotton dress and throw it over my body. I walk back to the living room and head off straight to the kitchen where mum is eagerly waiting for my belated evening greetings. Mum gets upset if I return home or any body for that matter who comes home and walks through the house without greeting her. So, I cheerfully call out "Hey mum, are you alright?" Mulishani ba mayo?

Mum is looking at me Up-down! Up-down! I jokingly, say, what is wrong mum, why are you not talking to me, and why are you looking at me up-down; up-down; have I done anything wrong to annoy you? Mum goes "uuugh" then she shrugs her shoulders and say, "Cinshi mwafwalila ilaya ilipi?" (Why are you wearing a short dress?) I am thinking mum has sworn to me that she can't see, how come she blames me for wearing a short dress? I decide to answer her back point blank. I say to her, but mum you always tell me you have gone blind and that you can not see a thing! How do you know I am wearing a short dress? (Imwe mayo mwanjeba ati tamumona iyoo, inga mwaishiba shani ati imfwele ilaya ilipi? Mum ignores my accusation and amid smiles she says, "Ala ulamoneka bwino inga wafwala filya ifimalaya ifi tali" (You look nice when you wear those long dresses (caftans)) I just burst out laughing! I am thinking it is no use trying to argue with mum over her sight so the two of us start laughing. I exaggerate my displeasure at not being allowed to wear short dresses and whinge to her by saying, ooh mum, you do not allow me to wear shorts and now you are telling me off for wearing a short dress, what do you expect me to wear when it is hot? (Imwe ba mayo mulanda ati nilafwala utuputula nomba mwatampa nokunkanya ukufwala indeleshi ishipi, inga nakulafwala finshi inga nakukaba). I think mum found my whinging funny because she kept smiling to herself.

However, Del (Katongo's four year old niece) was not so lucky because mum's poor eye sight almost ended in tragedy. Not being able to differentiate between a four year old girl and a dog, mum almost whacked up Del with her walking stick. Del who had been sent to bring a plate to my house walked in an un suspecting trap and was almost flattened by mum who was wildly swinging her walking stick aimed at her.

Apparently, mum had been ear-dropping over my anxieties and those of other tenants living on the complex over the vicious dogs being kept by my immediate neighbour. She had therefore inhibited strange fears of being attacked by dogs from next door.

With hind sight, we all agreed and appreciated the fact that our neighbours' dogs were to a certain extent an asset to our complex as they kept the would be burglars and thieves at our complex at bay. At the same time, neighbours craved for freedom whereby they could spend some evening hours basking in their well maintained front lawns and back gardens at will without the constant fear of being attacked by dogs. After all the complex is manned by a security guard (whose wages are being paid by tenants and not the landlord). So, as far as tenants are concerned that is enough protection and we hate the restrictions imposed on us by vicious dogs roaming our grounds once they escape or come out of their cage.

When I moved to this complex however, I was given the normal briefing by the landlord and the neighbour's dogs were mentioned at one stage although in a very positive manner. Up to the present day, nobody warned me that there was also an unwritten rule that tenants should not venture outside their homes after 9 p.m. I later learnt that dogs' cage is opened at 9 p.m. and dogs start roaming the complex at will until 5 or 6 a.m.

As though this is not enough, one evening, I was coming from a late appointment and my phone rang as I opened my kitchen back door. In the midst of answering my mobile phone and unlocking the door, I forgot to shut grill doors behind me and continued talking on the phone. Within seconds I heard this pudendum of dog's feet running on my kitchen veranda towards the open door. My instinct was to pull the grill door closed which is on the outside of the kitchen door. And for sure, as l had guessed the dog's head hit the grill door and the dog broke out into a big BARK! I just stood there trembling like a leaf! I kept imagining what would have happened to me had I not instinctively pulled the grill doors shut on time. I must confess the departure of the dog owners and their dogs from the complex a few months later brought joy to us all as we started having short morning walks in our lawns before retreating inside our homes to have a bath in readiness for the days' work engagements.

However, coming back to Del's narrow escape, mum had convinced Katongo to put the stool outside the flat and let her sit at the elms of the back garden to enjoy the morning sun shine. I am in my bedroom sorting out papers. All I hear is this loud shouting for help coming from outside. Mum is hysterically calling out for help. Mum goes "mutuleeee, mutuleeeee, mwebantu seni muntuleeee eeeeh! (Heeeelp! heeeelp! Heeeeelp, somebody help mee pleaseee).

I run out off my bedroom while Katongo throws away the shining brushes and cloths he had been using in polishing floors and runs after me. I am thinking, has mum fallen down or has she been attacked outside by dogs. Before I know it, I am on the kitchen veranda overlooking the back garden. And there, is mum vigorously waving her walking stick towards Del who is standing completely stunned and frozen! The girl is just gazing at mum her eyes bugled out and her mouth dropped and still holding on to the plate in her hands.

I hastily shout at mum and say "Imwe ba mayo Cinshi mulecita?" Mum, what are you doing? Mum calls out, imbwa! Imbwa! Imbwa shalansuma! (Dogs, Dogs, Dogs are coming to bite me) I say, mum, there are no dogs there! It is a little girl—Del! You know Katongo's niece don't you? Mum stops shouting and drops her walking stick, she then looks around her in puzzlement. I walk down to her and calmly say, what is the matter, did you mistake Del for a dog? (Mayo Cinshi, bushe mwacimona Del ati ni mbwa?) Mum says in a whisper "yes" I thought the dogs had come to attack me". (Nacimona ati imbwa shaisa mukunsuma).

I sit down with mum on the stool and ask Katongo to bring her a glass of cold water. At this point, my heart goes to the little girl standing before us and I feel she equally needs comforting. I leave mum still sitting on the stool and goes to embrace Del in my arms. I am all the time thinking that Del is going to burst out in tears at any given time, but she just looks at me still in a stance. I say to Katongo after I handed over the plate to him please Katongo can you fetch some sweets and crisps for Del. Katongo runs back in the house and brings the goodies and hands them over to the smiling Del. I then ask him to escort Del back to their servants' quarters while I continue chatting and comforting my mum.

However, it was a few hours later that I telephoned my baby sister and told her about Del's escape. Oh boy! Didn't we laugh! Some of the words couldn't come out of my mouth as I informed my sister, that mum should have been judged with GBH (grievous bodily harm) for hitting a minor by this time we are talking on the phone. My sister goes, WHAT? What did mum do? By the time I finished telling her what had happened, I was wiping tears from my eyes and I am sure my sister was doing the same thing. It must have been a terrifying experience for poor Del.

In line with psychological theory on conquering phobias, (desensitisation theory) I invited Del to come and be snapped with my mum and in the other snap holding mum's walking stick. She agreed with the blessings of her parents. I did not want Del to grow up fearing old people or their walking sticks.

STAY BLESSED DEL!!!

2011 CHRISTMAS TURMOIL

IT IS DECEMBER 2011. I am confused and wildly undecided.

On the positive side, a 40 foot container full of my household goods has arrived from England. For the first time in almost six months, my mum and I have all basic furniture and kitchen utensils. As icing on the cake, we also have a plasma TV plus a couple of HIFI systems. We are really living in luxury. One of the cases in the container is full of Xmas decorations, most of them preserved from previous Christmases and a few additional ones picked up from various one pound shops in London and Essex.

Despite my jubilant mood, there is a persistent little voice in my head which is continuously saying "hypocrite", "hypocrite". Am I an hypocrite I keep asking myself quietly. Why did I bring all these Xmas decorations and yet I cannot bring myself to buying a Xmas tree and decorating it as those were my intentions of packing a case full of Xmas decorations. These plans were arranged and sealed whilst on a short holiday in England during the period August/September 2011 and yet it is only December and my mind is already changed.

I may sound vain, but I am divided between spending Xmas with my mother in Zambia and probably give her the best festival time she has ever dreamt off or spend it with my family in England.

By the first week of December, my mind is made up based on two different factors both of which have been arrived at through their individual merits.

In the first place, mum is savaged by on-set dementia and may not even be able to tell the difference between Xmas day and any other ordinary day. I am thinking that I may go all out preparing Xmas day and waste a lot of money and effort for a day which may mean nothing to my mum and this may result in my having a very flat, lonely and frustrating Christmas for myself. I have noticed during the short period I have been in Zambia, especially with my immediate family, that they are reluctant to come for a meal or any sort of come together dinner. It is surprising that they run to attend funerals or marital conflicts. Has this got something to do with ego dominance or it is just implanted in the culture that family get together should only be at funerals and conflict solving meetings. Funny enough, they ignore illnesses, or relatives' hospitalisation and only wait for funeral gatherings, what a waste of time, effort and money. Could it be an inferiority complex issue or punishable vengeance similar to the famous Biblical Parable of "The Great Banquet" Luke Chapter 14 Versus 16-24.

On reflection, I have implanted in my children the strong cultural value and belief that Christmas comes only once a year and as such, should be regarded as a merry and joyous time for the family. It marks the birth of our Lord Jesus Christ who died for our Sins (Matthew 1 versus 18-24) This is how I was brought up. I am talking about a Zambian Christmas, where as children we wore new dresses and new shoes and ate lots of chicken and rice curry while indulging in Street parties. This is the way I celebrate my Christmas wherever I am on Planet Earth. Have you heard of an analogy which says: "You can get a person out of the ghetto, but you cannot get a ghetto out of them". A famous writer once wrote "I intend to live in the past because most of my life is there". Despite my age, and the fact that living in foreign lands meant being expected to get assimilated into different cultures, I still strongly feel connected to the life I led in a Zambian Village which I proudly look at as my cornerstone in my life. Hence I value Christmas and I endeavour and look forward to having a merry and joyous Christmas each year.

I therefore struggled to having a boring or flat 2011 Christmas in the absence of my family. These emotions were so strong that one day I just walked into a Travel Agent's office and inquired on current British Airways fares to London. I found a very friendly sales lady who actually advised that, reduced fares were closing on that very day and that increased December fares will be introduced the following day. To make matters worse, she advised that the dateline for reduced fares is 15.30 hours that very day. I had to think fast, I cancelled any other plans and raced to the bank to withdraw enough money to pay for a ticket to London. Fortunately, I was booked on 22/12/2011 flight. With an air ticket in my hand bag I felt like Xmas had even come and I was walking on planet Nine.

However, my happiness was short-lived. As I drove home I started thinking of how I may break news of my impending trip to mum. I knew that she would bemoan and jump to conclusions that I have also abandoned her. The second hassle was the realisation that I had not even unpacked my household goods from London which were still in boxes and suitcases scattered all over the place. Firstly I made up my mind that the London trip should be kept secret from mum and workers until such time that I make concrete night care arrangements for mum. I also decided to put all unpacked boxes and suitcases in both my own bedroom and the third bedroom until such time when I return back from my Xmas Holiday.

As regards to mum's care, I decide to telephone my young sister despite the fact that we have kept a deliberate silence for almost four weeks. As mentioned before, my siblings expect me to care for mum and give an everyday up-date on her condition. I feel, they are taking liberties with me and I sometimes prefer to concentrate on mum's care and leave other things to take care of themselves. I feel, I genuinely want to care for mum but her other children should also take responsibility even if it means ringing her once a week just to find out how she is getting on. Wouldn't mum do the same for them? Despite her dementia mum is continuously asking after her children. We usually keep secret, news of sickness in the family as mum becomes so distressed and wants to be with whoever is not well.

However, I pick up the phone and dial my sister's number, she answers almost immediate. I cheerfully say, Hi! How are things with you? Sometimes one has to swallow a bitter pill in order to get what she wants. I always remember what one senior diplomat told me whilst working at the Zambian Embassy in London. Apparently this diplomat was so disgruntled and did not mind sharing his discomfort and frustration with a locally engaged staff. This man lamented and looked over where I was sitting typing away my work. He said to me, "You know what political life is so fraughtful sometimes it feels like sleeping in a room full of snakes". Nobody likes the slippery devious characters, I thought. Is he talking about sleeping with an enemy? I looked at him and saw the anguish on his face, unfortunately, those days I was not even properly qualified to comfort the poor man. All I said was, 'do not worry, things might change for the better'.

What I am trying to say is that 'life' in general is very fraughtful. It is not just political life which is difficult, even dealing with own siblings can be as painful as though you are confronting an enemy. Anyway on this occasion I did not give my baby sister any chances, I simply grabbed the ox by it's horns before the phone cut off or before I developed cold feet. I deliberately lowered my voice and said, I am just ringing to find out if you may look after mum while I am away over the Christmas period. I quickly add and say, the two workers will be here but mum needs to be with somebody at night as she is scared of spending a night on her own.

My sister's voice goes cold. She is really struggling with words. The first thing she says is "How about Anne?" (Anne is a niece I pay to assist with mum's care). I answer back almost angrily, I say, Anne is a married woman with three young children. I further state that Anne works during the day and goes back to care for her family in the evenings.

My sister detects the anger in my voice and says in an almost whisper that, "I can only assist if mum is brought to live with us on the Copper Belt" I am almost dropping my phone as my hand is shaking violently. I am thinking, what kind of a daughter is this? Mum is almost 90 years old. She is ravaged with dementia and she is usually confused, frightened and disoriented. How could she embark on a journey travelling back to the Copper Belt seeking somebody to care for her.

Having said so, my sister knows that even before the on-set of mum's dementia she has a fear of travelling. Mum's fears are so bad that they have manifested themselves into a phobia. Mum would go on self-imposed fasting for days before she undertakes any journey. She is afraid of vomiting or asking to go to the toilet whilst travelling. Can anybody believe that such simple natural activities which all of us travellers take for granted are mum's most feared huddles in her entire life. I couldn't therefore understand how my sister could even contemplate the thought of myself despatching mum on a coach en route to the copper belt, a journey which may take up to six or seven hours. I, for one would not like to put my mother through such an excruciating experience for her again.

However, I was left flabbergasted and shell shocked. I did not even make an effort of responding to my sister's suggestion but just reminded her of my departure date and rang off. My sister did not call me back but I managed to make own arrangements with the help of my niece Anne who agreed to move in my house with her two youngest children.

On Wednesday evening, 21ˢᵗ December, 2011 I sit down with mum and explain to mum that I will be away for three weeks as I intend to visit my children in England. Mum mumbles something then she looks at me and says, I should only stay away for two days. (Ukekale fye inshiku shibili). Then mum goes into her imaginary world and starts talking about how she feels abandoned by her own children. She says you have also left me alone (Naiwe wanshya neka). Before my emotions kick in, I say to mum, "look here, I have a small present for you" I open my pulse and pull out two K50,000 notes. I tell her this is your Christmas present. I will bring some more presents for you when I come back from England. This money I tell her is for your SDA Church offering. Mum's face brightens up and she is asking how much money I have given her. "Mwambela shinga impiya?" I say to mum I have given you One Hundred Thousand Kwacha (Namipela amwanda umo). Mum folds the two K50,000 notes and ties them on the corner of her chitenge material. I feel good that mum is happy although I am dreading the morning good-byes.

Come Thursday morning, 22nd December, 2011, I pack up my travelling bag, call for a taxi, say my good byes to mum and Anne and I am on my way to Kenneth Kaunda International Airport at 6.30 a.m. I already feel I am on holiday. Mind you, this is Zambia, at 6.30 a.m. the sun is high up in the sky and I am awashed with the beautiful morning sun rays at the back of the car. I am thinking, Good Lord, this is an escape from this entangled fraught existence. Hey, do not get me wrong, I am very keen and totally committed to caring for mum but my siblings' attitude towards mum's care triggers a flow of bile into my mouth.

Nine or ten hours later, I land at London's Heathrow Airport. God, it feels like coming back home. I feel pleased and light hearted. I pass through customs like lightening. I am constantly visualizing the faces of my little angels (grand children). I am already quietly debating on what presents to get for each one of them. I am imagining their usual loving

Words on opening presents of "Thank you very much grandma". Oh, I love to hear such words from my grand children and I am already smiling to myself as I walk along the long airport passages leading to "Arrivals Waiting Lounges".

My youngest son who lives in West London picks me up and drives me to my eldest son's house in Gidea Park, Essex. My son and his family are away on a pre-Christmas short break in Wales. I am already aware of their absence and I feel great to have the house to myself for a change. I feel I will be able to draw up my Christmas presents list and even do some shopping without any interruptions.

However, I will be cheating if I do not mention the excitement I felt when I entered my son's house at the decor and the number of presents heaped at the Christmas tree. Like a child, I went straight to the Christmas tree and started going through presents picking the ones addressed to me. I sit down and smilingly I am feeling and guessing what is in each box or present. In the meantime my son is just standing watching me. I realise, I must do something to toast Xmas festival with my son. I stand up and walk to the kitchen, I pull out two glasses and go into my bag where I had packed two Baileys bottles which I had bought at the Airport Duty Free shop I poured out the drink and gave one glass to my son and took the remaining one. We simultaneously raised our glasses and said "HAPPY CHRISTMAS" to each other.

A few hours later, my son drives back to West London. I decide to retire to bed early. I also woke up early probably the Zambian time still clicking in my head (two hours ahead of winter U.K. time). I take a quick bath and head off to South East London to meet my Luapula clique Mrs Magdalene Chibangu. She is a very good friend of mine and we have been friends for a long time. (My policy has always been to keep old friends. New friends may sometimes be tricky) I have friends I met at primary and secondary schools—forty or so years ago and those are my true friends. Magdalene is my sister in-waiting. When I mourn she mourns with me. When I am happy, she is also happy. I remember going through a very nasty patch and Magdalene was there for me. The two of us embarked on sending scud missiles (sharp Luapula words) to this person who was abroad at the time of his offense. We won the battle leaving the wounded rat miserable and footless. The rest is history.

Whilst in South London I decide to put a call through to my sister. We exchange pleasantries and I emphasise the fact that I am already in London. And that I have heard from Anne that mum is expressing difficult behaviours probably after realizing that I am away. I politely ask her if she can go and assist in caring for mum in my absence. My sister seems concerned this time and says she will consult and see if she can travel to Lusaka the following week by Wednesday, 28/12/2011. "Nalaipusha" (I will ask or consult) I am still holding my phone thinking, for goodness sake this is an emergency, anybody would see the need for her presence in Lusaka. Now I am puzzled with the word she has used "Nalaipusha". Did mum consult anybody to have her? What kind of person would not allow somebody to attend to a demented parent? Is my sister being controlled by dark forces? I know she is a very caring person what has gotten her. Since I arrived back in Zambia her behaviour has been erratic, aversive and fearful.

I am thinking caring for mum should not be solely my responsibility especially if there are other siblings to assist wherever necessary. I am a returnee who is desperately trying to establish herself back home. They are already settled in their own ways. What makes them think I am the slave driver? They cannot simply offload mum on me single handed. My anguish goes far as there is no help from the Government. I have not heard any debates nor having heard of any projects set for the care of the elderly in Zambia. I am actually finding myself at the end of my tether. One minute I am happy that I came back home to care for mum the other minute I am regretting this decision which has thrown me into untold despair.

Coming back to my Christmas Day the first thing I did was to telephone Anne to find out how mum was. I gave instructions on what to cook and what to dress mum in and I felt I had fulfilled my duties regarding mum's care.

Having said so, my Christmas Day in England was fabulous, I gave and I also received beautiful presents. We ate, danced and played games till late. With my Zambian time still ticking in my brains I retired to bed around 12 Midnight which was 2 a.m. for me. I was told the following day that the young ones with strong bones and muscles stayed up until 3 a.m. British time. When I woke up, on 26/12/2011 I discovered that there was still plenty of food and drinks to spoil myself with. Then I realised I had pending invitations for Boxing Day Dinners.

Feeling satisfied and taking on board my new given title of "the best grandma in the World", I sat down and congratulated myself that I made the right decision to spend 2011 Christmas with my family back in England.

PILLOW TREASURES

I AM IN MY BEDROOM reading my favourite book "Strength within" written by Barbra Hansen. I hear mum calling me by the name "Chengo" which surprises me. Mum and dad have always called me "Bupe" which is direct translation to Grace.

With mum's blessings and after a request to buy her a new blanket and a new pair of canvas shoes which I obediently did, I got her approval to start using her 4th generation ancestor's name 'Chengo'. I love the name Chengo and I admire the rugs to riches story behind this remarkable woman's life.

Anyway mum calls out again, mayoo, ba Chengo eeeh, eeeh! I know deep down that this flattery is up to something. What does mum want from me I quietly ask myself. Mayoo, eeeh! I answer back, yes mum! She says mpeniko akaluyembe (give me a razor blade). I am thinking, am I hearing mum properly, what is the razor blade for? I call out to her and say, what is the razor blade for mum? I want to cut my nails mum says. I say to her but you can't see properly how are you going to use the razor blade without cutting yourself? Mum says her nails have grown so long, they resemble the birds' crows. In order to avoid any agitation I say to mum, I have a nail filer which you can use to shorten your nails. I get off my bed and take the nail filer to mum and I show her how to use it. Apparently, mum gets fascinated with the artily of filing nails. Hence she puts the filer under her pillow making it the first treasure in her possession.

Mum's second sacred possession under her pillow is a small pocket bible. As it happened, my cousin visited from Mufulira. This lady is a devout Christian and she kept Evangelising to mum. One morning she asked me if I had a bible in the house. I told her all my bibles are still in transit with other household goods but then I said to her I have a small English pocket bible. She asked me to fetch it which I did. My cousin goes to mum "put this bible under your pillow and you will never have any night mares or bad dreams. My mum grabbed the small bible, placed the nail filer in between pages and placed it under her pillow. That bible joined her treasures under the pillow.

Mum places two of her many chitenge materials under her pillow. At first I could not understand her actions and we used to have big fights every morning for removing her citenges and placing them in the airing cupboard which I thought was the right place for them. Mum could get angry with me and request that I place them under her pillow. Them one morning while making up her bed, I carefully inspected the chitenge materials and realised that she had tied some money notes on them. I was surprised because I thought mum keeps her money in the jewellery box. But then I realised that each time mum is given money (I am not sure whether it is a Zambian or an African tradition to occasionally give something to an old relative during visits) Mum gets small amounts from generous relatives especially grandchildren which she keeps for her SDA weekly offerings. Mum treasures these monies and only a few selected individuals are permitted to touch or let alone count her monies. I have excluded myself from getting involved in mum's monies as she used to moan over missing money.

However, trouble starts when she thinks her money has gone missing, then all of us become suspects (myself and my domestic workers). In frustration, I sometimes go in her room and look around and occasionally find same missing money or envelop hidden somewhere but she had forgotten where she had put it. I got fade up and asked her to take stock of her loot. This is the same money she ties on corners of her chitenge materials which she places under her pillow. Occasionally when one of her trustees pops round, she unties the money and together they count the money and thereafter transfer the money into mum's jewellery box. It is a painstaking exercise which I could not tolerate. It was not only counting which got to me, it was the consistent questioning which followed immediately I stepped in the house from wherever I had been during the day. Mum could start firing questions on my arrival such as: How much did you put away in the jewellery box? How much is this week's offering? Who untied my chitenge and took the money? How many people know where

I put my money? I started loosing patience with her in the end I just thought enough is enough and I told her I did not want to get involved with her monies. I make up mum's bed every morning but I leave what is under her pillow untouched. I do not allow workers to make mum's bed for fear of misplacing her pillow treasures.

JANUARY BLUES

IT IS WEDNESDAY MORNING, 11TH January 2012 and I am still in England. The Xmas and New Years' festivals are just winding down. People are now obsessed of loosing extra pounds piled on through self indulgence of Xmas meals. Another obsession stem from the January sales which are accelerated by enticing down priced images of goods on television and are beckoning night and day.

However, with regards to my family we have one more date to celebrate before the 2011 chapter is closed and put behind us. The 12th day of January, marks the day when myself and my husband became parents for the first time. I still remember, 38 years on how I dreaded looking at my baby boy when nurses thrashed him on my laps after his birth. I was scared of so many things, I thought I might pass on my average looks on him. I was also afraid of holding him in case I break his fragile bones.

Having said so, I grew up with a fixation on babies but only when they are aged six months and over as this is the time when babies are cuddly and firm to handle. My parents belonged to Watch Tower Sect where my father was the Elder and there were several conferences and large gatherings at our house as well as Sunday Services. At such gatherings I enjoyed going round picking up and carrying babies on my back. I must admit, baby carrying for me was an escape route from attending the prolonged, repetitive and restrictive Bible Lessons (equivalent to Sunday School) for children. My well thought through strategy was to pick on a crying baby, and with the help of an adult I could throw and strip it on my back and run outside dancing and chanting to the baby until it falls asleep.

Whilst in the process of writing this chapter, my elder brother came to recuperate at my house after an illness. He started helping me with some of my childhood stories which I could not remember myself. On my fascination for babies, he informed me that apart from picking and running around with babies belonging to church members, I also used to make my own babies from clay moulds. He further informed that I used to give my mud dolls real names. He remembers how I named most of my dolls "Chitembeya". My brother nor myself could not think of a reason why I gave this name to my babies.

Coincidently, both my brother and myself agreed that the route which our family took on frequent church trips passed through Chitembeya village. I remember as a child probably aged about three or four being placed closely to another sibling on a bicycle carrier and passing through this village where people greeted us very warmly. Could it be my parents had relatives at Chitembeya village or as a child I became influtauted by the name Chitembeya? Unfortunately my father is dead and my mother is savaged by dementia and is unable to help me with the Chitembeya saga nor their connections to it.

Coming back to my baby boy, at the age of 20 when my first child was born, I was still not confident about my looks. I only came to realise about my beauty in my early 30s, 40s and let alone in my 50s when I started enjoying and flourishing the attention and compliments I was getting. On reflection, I actually created a vicious cycle in that I married early aged 19 and naturally I rebuked male admirers as a married woman. At the same time I felt unattractive as male admirers kept their distance from me apart from a few determined ones whose advances were subtle and mostly went unnoticed by me.

Things changed when I went to University in my early thirties and got exposed and became more confident within myself. For example whilst working as a social worker at Camden Social Services, in North London I was all the time likened to Mrs Winnie Mandela—it was like, hey boy, me looking like the beautiful Winnie Mandela—whaah! Whaah! I jokingly protested and used to say I do not come from South Africa, I am Zambian hence Winnie is not even my distant auntie nor cousin and how could I inherit her vivacious looks?

And believe you me! Upon my return to Zambia in 2011 and especially after the new Government came to Power in September, 2011, I am mistaken for Hon. Prof. Nkandu Luo—It happened three times in Lusaka. The first time was my own baby brother. One morning, we stopped at Long Acres ATM in Lusaka, so that I could draw some money. With my back to the car, I over-heard my brother calling me. I thought somebody was trying to steal from me and I quickly backed off the ATM machine. With a big smile plastered all over my brother's face he started pointing at this woman who was by then emerging from a Chemist. I could not make sense of what he was saying. He seemed so excited and he kept pointing in the same direction. I said to him angrily, what is the matter? He says, look at that woman who looks like you. I said, which one? I looked where my brother was pointing and saw this nicely dressed woman who by then was surrounded by one or two people who were greeting her. My brother says, that is Professor Nkandu Luo. I protested and said, I do not look like her, thank you, very much and I laughed off. I then walked back to the ATM to finish my transaction. The other two incidents took place at Filling Stations in Lusaka where two men on separate occasions left their cars to come and greet me thinking I was Hon. Nkandu Luo. I just laughed and thought—ooh dear, "I wish I had Professor Luo's brains and courage".

The third incident took place in London. On 22nd January 2012 I was at London's Heathrow Airport awaiting a Lusaka bound British Airways flight. As I sat with my grand daughter, my son and his partner chatting away, I saw this black man coming directly to where we were sitting with a big glen on his face, he started bowing down left, right and centre, the four of us just watched in puzzlement. I suspected this man's motives but I kept quiet. When he reached where we were he said in Bemba with his head bowed down "Ooh ba Honourable, bushe elyo mulebwelela kumushi?" (Ooh honourable Lady, is this the time when you are returning back home?) I looked round to make sure Honourable Prof. Luo was not anywhere near me, then I answered the man in Bemba and said "Nibani mulelanda nabo" (Whom are you speaking to?) Then he looked up and said, ooh, sorry, are you not Hon Professor Nkandu Luo? I said no, I am not. I am actually, Mrs . . . .) the gentleman looks up and fixes a glance at me and then he says: "Ooh Mrs . . . . I did not realise you look so much like Prof. Luo and where have you been? We do not see you around London these days. How is Mr . . . . it is such a long time since I last saw you. My god you look exactly like Prof Nkandu Luo". In the meantime, my son and his family had no clue about what was going on until the gentleman left laughing and I told them Hon. Prof. Luo is a cabinet Minister in the Zambian government. My son goes, "Ooh that's not bad mum" and my daughter in-law goes "whaa! Whaa" Unfortunately my eight year old grand daughter had no clue about this strange encounter she just watched us laughing.

In short, what I am saying is, I shouldn't have been so worried about my baby's likeness to my looks if at 35 I am likened to Winnie Mandela and in my fifties I look like Hon. Prof. Luo, definitely there must be some germ looks in me!. I guess, I am ageing graciously and I have no complaints about my looks now.

Coming back to my childbirth, just one glance at my baby resolved all my unanswered questions. He was such a charmer, my baby was so stunning!!. He just looked so perfect, he was like made to perfection. In fact, his looks has never faded in his adulthood. For example, when my son was at University in England he had such good looks and girls referred to him as the "African Prince". As evidence of his assumed royalty he got hooked on with the most attractive girl at the campus (a model and singer) and they wedded a few years later. Each time I look at my grandchildren—the product of this reunion, I feel like I am browsing through the OK Magazine which is full of brushed down photos of children of film stars. I am sure my grand children's good looks stem from both parents. I cherish and love my grand children to bits. Of course I feel proud, who knows probably they have inherited those good looks from my lineage of the family tree.

Coming back to my January blues, I am sitting in bed thinking of what present to get for my son's birthday. I am debating whether to buy something or just give him a little cash. Before I even reach any conclusion, the phone starts ringing, I turn over and think, this is a little early. It's just gone 06.30 a.m. then I rub my eyes and tell myself that it is 08.30 a.m. in Zambia. I feel the missed call is no good and decide to get a rest and psych myself up for whatever is coming from Zambia. Before I even close my eyes, another missed call registers on my mobile phone. I sit up in bed and noisely graunt to my self. I grab the phone and say, "this is it, I must call back now". I am shaking, my heart is doing its jumps in my mouth, and I keep thinking mum must have fallen ill in the night or something really nasty has happened back home.

I hold my breath and redial the number. On two rings I hear a familiar voice. Hello Auntie the voice says. I am thinking, please tell me now, what is the matter. However, in a very controlled voice I ask, is everything alright Ann? She answers me and says "yes Auntie", in my heart I am thinking, why are you putting through missed calls to me at this time of the morning if everything is alright. Outwardly I say, alright then, and what are your calls for? Ann says, everything is alright, it is just that Auntie left (referring to my young sister who had been taking care of mum while I was on a Xmas short break in England). I repeat her words and say why has your auntie left my house. Ann pauses and does not answer me directly. I am getting angry and I bark at her and say, can you tell me why your auntie has left my house now! She stammers and says—"Awee kwali efyongo". (There were some misunderstandings). I am now at the point of shouting, I answer back and say, misunderstandings with who? And what has that got to do with mum?

At this point my heart sinks. I am feeling nausea. I am thinking this is not alright. My sister cannot leave my house without telling me. Who is going to care for mum at night. Why shouldn't she ring me? And what state is mum in? Does mum know her favourite baby daughter has abandoned her? I am trying hard not to sound angry nor scared as I speak to Ann. I start again and say, Ann can you tell me the reason why my sister left. Did you have a quarrel? Ann goes, no, Auntie started complaining that she wants to go and see her husband on the copper belt that she has stayed for two weeks and wants to get back home. I say to Ann I spoke to my sister the other day when I sent housekeeping money and she never mentioned anything about going back to see her husband. Ann goes, Auntie was not happy that you mentioned something about going to Manchester before you return back to Zambia. I say to Ann, yes I would have gone to Manchester for a day but I changed my mind altogether and I will not go. I am thinking why should my day visit to Manchester scare my sister? How far does she think Manchester is from London? Has she got any idea of transport facilities in England. Of course she is oblivious to the fact that I can fly to Manchester and would be there in less than an hour. I can use fast train that can take me almost two and half hours or I can use a coach which may take me five or six hours. In my heart I am not seeing any connection between my trip to Manchester and my niece's and sister's quarrel in Zambia.

However, I detected some hesitation in Ann's explanation and pushed on rather tentatively to find the main cause of my sister's sudden departure. As far as I was concerned, I could not afford to scare Ann or upset her in any way as she is my only lifeline between mum being left on her own without any help in the night or go back to the drawing board and ask Ann to move in my house with her two youngest children until I return back home. I coax Ann, half pleading that she should tell me what the problem is so that I can make plans for mum's care for the remaining two weeks before my eventual return back home. Ann goes, yes, we had a quarrel and Auntie was insulting me and she decided to leave. I said but you know that you should not exchange bitter words with adults especially your aunties (Ann is our first cousin's daughter) hence she is our blood relative. Ann goes, but auntie told me off and said she will bring in another person to care for grandma.

I start panicking, I can literally feel blood running through my veins. I visualise the thought that I had just offloaded a container full of household goods which I had stacked into spare bedrooms and to have a stranger in the house would be like "tying a goat in a green maize field". Where am I going to get replacement goods if my stuff is stolen? I swallow hard and tell myself to calm down and get control of the situation.

I am almost speaking to myself when I recover from my trance, I huskily ask Ann, are you still there? She says yes auntie! I say to her, listen very carefully to what I am going to tell you. Go home and ask your husband if he can permit you to move into my house with your two youngest children like you did on my departure. I also ask Ann if there was enough food at home. She said Auntie bought us some meat before she left. I said don't worry I will send some money via Western Union when I go to the bank today. As for now, leave mum with Katongo and go home and do as I have told you. Goodbye!!

I am still furious and I am shaking. Have I wakened people in the house? I ask myself. I put my head on the pillow and remain silent for a few minutes, the house is still quiet but my heart is almost tearing off my chest as it speeds up with it's summer sautés. I keep telling myself to calm down and to quickly come up with plan two.

Who on earth is going to help me with this dilemma. I count my friends in Zambia. I have two or three childhood friends. Can I call them now? I tell myself not to. These can only help in an emergency where I fail to remit cash back home at short notice for whatever reason maybe due to bank holidays or something like that. You do not ask friends to abandon their husbands to go and nurse your demented mother at night. Far from it—that would be equivalent to asking for a cup of tea with the Queen.

Then I remember the vivacious Grace Lumaka (my husband's first cousin). I dial her number and she answers at the first ring. I say to her, Grace listen, I have a problem at my house in Makeni. My sister has left to attend to an emergency on the copper belt (a small white lie). Then I gather courage and say, is it possible for you to care for my mother during night time? As an after thought I say to Grace please do not forget to get permission from your husband. I also mentioned that Ann will do the first two nights and thereafter I would like you to take over and that I will pay for your service. Grace agrees without any hesitation. She says "Ba mulamo I will do it I am sure ba shi Mambwe will allow me to sleep at your house while I care for ba pongoshi" I felt relieved, and for the first time in those forty minutes or so, I had been on the phone I smiled to myself and felt good. Then I thought what reward can I give to this sweet sister in-law? I calmly say to Grace—I am remitting some house-keeping money in your name and you need to distribute funds as per my instructions. I gave details of how money should be used. Grace was over the moon.

I must admit, I have a soft spot for Grace who does not only share a same Christian name with me but who appears to be my favourite from my husband's family. I looked after Grace at my house when she was a young girl. As I was not good at speaking nor understanding Kaonde (my husband's language) Grace used to translate to me what my in-laws or let alone any other relative said about me. This was of great help to me, mind you this is about thirty nine years ago when marrying a man or woman from a different tribe in Zambia was viewed as inappropriate especially from the man's family. The wife from another tribe was criticised for everything from cooking, to shining the house floors and not forgetting dress sense. Even if one had to dress up for office work (in-laws expected a daughter in-law to wear a chitenge "wrapper" on top of a dress or skirt). Apparently, in the eyes of my in-laws, I came from a wrong tribe "Bemba" which by then was perceived as a tribe of out-spoken women. Don't get me wrong, there are certain traditional expectations which cannot be fulfilled by a working woman. Things like applying cobra to tiles or wooden floors and shining them while bent on two knees. What is wrong in paying somebody to carry on such domestic chores and concentrate on more sophisticated duties like meal preparations, probably nurturing and feeding babies etc. Can a wife be termed lazy for not shining house floors, especially if she goes out to work and brings in reasonable income in the household.

However, despite everything, the Kaonde man was my hero in waiting. He took me to England, he witnessed both my educational and professional developments and most importantly he has fathered my four beautiful and intelligent children. What else can I ask from the Kaonde people? They have given me priceless gifts and I will forever remain indebted to them.

As for my January Blues, Grace, Ann and Katongo helped in caring for mum night and day until I finally returned back home on 23rd January, 2012. As regards to my young sister who abandoned mum, I did not telephone her whilst in London but I made a point of facing her personally. I drove to her shop on 24th January and asked her to give me her reasons for abandoning mum at the time when I was away. Our discussion was quite fruitful, my sister profusely apologised to me and promised to apologise to mum. I am still waiting for mum's apology to be delivered.

On my part I have accepted my baby sister's apology and I have forgiven her, it goes without saying "SISTERS WILL ALWAYS BE SISTERS"!!!

MUM AND A MAN IN A WHITE COAT

MYSELF AND MUM ARE SITTING on our verandah enjoying the late afternoon sunshine. I come up with a little conversation just to cheer her up. I tactfully inquire and say to her, mum I hear you were taken to a clinic while I was away. Mum goes aada! I coax her and say, mum please tell me about your illness and your encounter with a man dressed in a white coat. Mum shifts on the stool where she is sitting while I squat on the floor by her side. Mum ignores what I am asking her, she looks at me and says I told you I want to go inside the house I do not want to sit outside any more. "Ninkweba ati ndefwaya ukwingila mung'anda pano nshipatemenwe iyoo".

I am thinking, why this change of temperament. Mum was fine a while ago and now she seems to have changed into a bad mood. After all it is her who insisted that she wanted to sit in the sun and I took a stool outside for her. Anyway I guessed I touched a wrong subject maybe my questioning upset her. Actually both my sister and brother had already informed me about mum's encounter with a male doctor who attended to her at the clinic. I laughed so much when the story was narrated to me hence I desperately wanted to hear it being told by mum herself.

After noticing that mum was very nervous and did not want to talk about her visit to the clinic, I changed my line of questioning and said: "By the way mum, what medicine were you given at the clinic where my brother took you. Mum looks down and says: "Nikwisa naile?" (Where did I go?) I repeat myself and say, mum you were taken to a clinic by my brother when you fell ill that time I was away. Mum seems to concentrate on whatever she is thinking probably she is trying hard to remember the events I am talking about, then she turns to look at me and firmly says: "Limbi bakatukonkela pantu twalifyukile fye" (Probably, hospital staff will come after me as I did not go back after their assessment) I am thinking, good Lord, is this what is making mum feel so nervous to talk about her visit to the clinic because she thinks she escaped and they will come after her?

I am all the time trying to empathize with mum. How does one cope with a person like mum who is constantly scared of everything may it be a hospital doctor, nurse or policeman. I am trying to put myself into her place. How can I feel to operate in mum's world with such fears hanging on me? What makes mum think she escaped from the clinic? Didn't my brother explain the procedure to her or she just did not like the entire process. Then I decide to ask mum about staff. I say to mum, I hear a young male doctor attended to you, is it true?

(Naliumfwa ati doctor umwaume ewa mipimine) Mum bursts into a big smile and says "Ala eko twasebene uku" (I made a nuisance of myself) I am alarmed and I am imagining all these wild things happening to mum, I am thinking, did mum become incontinent of herself, did she vomit or fell asleep during the examination. I coax mum and say what did you do to embarrass yourself? Mum goes, "Kabili baebele ati pimpula Ishati, elyo batampa ukufinaula mumala, bushe tabakwata umucinshi" (He asked me to lift up my top, and then he started squeezing my tummy, that was not respectful) I said yes mum, that's what the doctor should do, he touches your tummy then he asks you where you feel the pain. Mum goes, no, no that man who was dressed in a white coat was only calling my name and I was answering back to him "yes sir" "yes sir". (Awee ulya umwaume uwafwele iceceti ilya buta elenjita fye ishina elyo ndeasuka ati "mukwai" "mukwai". I said to mum, listen mum the doctor must have been asking you whether you felt any pain when he touched your stomach. Mum smiled at me and said but he kept calling "Besa" and I answered him back "yes sir".

Despite mum's funny explanation, I am feeling sick and angry, I keep imagining mum being completely disorientated and confused. She actually deserved some translation or explanation regarding the medical procedure being carried on her. Were there no Bemba speaking personnel to translate at the clinic for her? I just felt something was not politically correct hence mum's fears of hospitals and doctors were accelerated and it is not only her, for any dementia sufferer would have experienced the same confusion.

Once again, it dawned on me that there is need to educate people on the treatment of the elderly—it is a category in our country which is lacking behind in accessing healthcare, and general recognition of their plight.

MUM'S FIXATION

I START A SMALL CHAT with mum. We are sitting in the kitchen where I have brought a stool for mum to sit on (anyway before the container of household goods arrived in Zambia, myself and mum had only one stool to share as house furniture). We had our own beds but had little or no furniture apart from cooker, fridge, four plates, two glasses two knives, two forks e.t.c. So the stool was sometimes the centre of heated disagreements. Mum wouldn't let me use the stool and she stubbornly requested that it should remain in her bedroom at all times.

Her selfish possessiveness genuinely angers me, dementia or no dementia. I feel, I deserve a right to my own possessions. I sometimes remind mum that I paid K500,000 at auction for this beautiful leather stool made in the shape of Africa. I loved the stool and was willing to pay even higher had it not been to my clever assistant cum driver who acted as another punter and made clever moves to offset other interested punters.

As though claiming my possessions is not enough, on her bad days, mum thinks I am one of the house workers and she commands me to obey her orders. For example one morning I sat in the kitchen typing away on my laptop. Apparently mum was looking for the stool which was not in her room as I was sitting on it in the kitchen. Around 7.15 a.m. mum walks in the kitchen fuming and without her walking stick. She stands and hooves over me and in an authoritative voice she says, why are you not sweeping the house? "Ninshi taulepyangila mu ng'anda?" "Lelo ndefwaya bonse muwamye ing'anda" (Today, I want all of you to clean the house up). I did not know whether to laugh or get angry. I just stood up after realising that I had forgotten to give mum her 7 a.m. cup of tea. In the meantime, mum looks round and sees the stool, she goes and sits in the middle of it completely blocking me out. Is'nt she clever? I boil water and give her a cup of tea and pick up my lap top and go back to continue typing in my bedroom while mum sits on the stool unaware of my anger and frustration. Poor mummy, her mind sometimes becomes so distorted and muddled up and she wouldn't even know who the boss is. She only cares about what matters to her, her assumed belongings, hey! give us a break mum, you've already taken over my social life, now you are also forbidding me access to my own possessions!!

However, with regards to mum's disorientation and anxiety panics, I prefer sitting with her whenever I am at home. It could be sitting together in the kitchen while I prepare meals or taking her into my bedroom while I type on the lap top. Being with mum prevents unnecessary searches and her persistent calling out for me. And once

I answer her calls and present myself in her bedroom, mum comes up with flimsy lame excuses. Mum sometimes gets frightened of anything. It could be un explained shadow (probably one of the workers may pass by her bedroom window and she sees his/her shadow and that may trigger a panic attack. What a waste of time! Once I am interrupted in my work through mum's calls, and by the time I get back to my typing, I have forgotten the trend of thought I was in and my work sometimes becomes muddled up.

Mum, I call out to her, how was your day? Mum keeps quiet then I try again. Mum, I thought my sister passed through today, did she stay for a long time? Mum shrugs her shoulders before answering me. I am thinking, does mum find it difficult to discuss my sister with me. Then I remember that I fore warned my sister not to make any unnecessary promises to visit mum which she cannot fulfil and I also advised her that during her visits to mum, she should stick to little simple chats with her and no heavy stuff at all. My sister as well as myself are sometimes in denial and takes mum to be the mother we had 20 or 10 years ago. Who wants to admit that their mother is ravaged by dementia and has lost her marbles? Even at the time of writing this book, I am hoping that one day I will wake up and have a reasonable discussion with my mother. I long to tell her all these problems I am having in caring for her, I want to pour my anger and frustration on her. But as days pass by my wishful thinking is fading away. Our present mother finds it difficult to retain information and has problems making sense of heavy discussions. Mum lacks concentration and sometime gets carried away with her distorted thoughts. I presumed the two of them must have had a chat during which time mum must have been told not to say anything about my sister's visit to me. As usual, I tell off myself for even contemplating a scenario which I was not part of. I do not like associating bad things to people especially my own blood I will always try to think of a positive perception to justify their inappropriate behaviours. I resent suffocating my heart and body with hatred. I pray to cleanse my body and enjoy life by engulfing my body and spirit in laughter, love and peace. I am not one to carry a chip on my shoulder. Amen!!

Coming back to my little chat with mum, I decide to change the subject and start telling her about a telephone call I received from one of my nieces. This Ms altitude had made a business trip to Mansa or that was what I was told. However, from the day she left, I started getting morning missed calls sometimes at 5.30 or 6 a.m. demanding for money to buy her business stuff (cater pillars). I got fade up and told her that I was not part of her business transaction as she had mentioned earlier that one of her cousins was purportedly sponsoring her. Anyway, on second thoughts and to maintain my peace of mind, I decided to send some money to her. So I am telling mum how after getting the money I sent through the Western Union this little madam called me (in short this cheek madam managed to buy talk time with the money I sent her) and started abusing me on the phone. I say to mum, mum I felt so insulted and got so angry over this person's selfish motives. I said, I told her off and put her back into her rightful place.

Mum shrugged her shoulders, moves a bit on the stool and says. "Inga ukabaposa kwisa?" "Ala ulebasulako fye". (Where are you going to take them, you should just ignore what they are saying). I am thinking—there is a lot of sense in what mum is saying, nevertheless, I have her to care for single-handedly. And these other people should be grateful rather than being abusive for the little help I am giving them. Anyway I kept quite—probably to show mum that I am still angry or just for respect when mum gives advice I keep quite. Actually of late I become emotional when mum makes a sensible statement because this is the mother I want. Probably I am engulfed in denial with regards to mum's current mental health condition. This is the mother I know who calms me down. Mum is very caring especially to her extended family. Mum has outlived all her siblings leaving her with the responsibility of caring for some of her siblings' needy off-springs. Mum took and still takes her responsibilities to her siblings' children very seriously. Unlike current trends where "family" is wife/husband and children (nucleus family) mum's generations' family was (extended family) it started from immediate family, then clan, then tribe. Oh dear, no wonder I've so many uncles, aunties, cousins and in-laws. It is a generation game! On mum's account, I still have relatives from her $5^{\text{th generation}}$ (ancestors).

Apparently, both of us (mum and me) are deep in our own thoughts. Then, out of the blue mum says "bushe wali mumonapo umwaice obe apo aishila?" (Have you seen/met your young sister since she came?) I am thinking, where is this chat taking us? However, I answer mum back and say, no, I have not met her yet. Then on second thoughts I say, but mum don't you realise that my sister only sneaks in briefly when she knows that I'm not around. If she really wants to meet me she should have made an effort to either ring me in advance or wait for me while she is at my house. Mum ignores my laments and says: "Awee naonda sana" (She has lost so much weight) why should my sister loose so much weight) I am sitting there thinking how do I respond to this motherly concern? Anyway I decide to make light of it and I say, why should my sister loose weight? (Ninshi oondele?) Mum gazes ahead of her as though she is really concentrating on giving her verdict. Then she turns to face me and she says "kabili abalume balilwala umuchele" (her husband suffers from salt disease) Mum! I exclaim, there is no such disease called 'salt disease' do you mean 'sugar disease? Mum says "Eeeh kabili mulamo obe eyo alwala" (your brother in-law suffers from that disease) I am now concealing my laughter and trying to reason with mum but I know deep down my heart that mum will swear upon my head (her daughter) that she knows my brother in-law suffers from salt disease. So I give in because I know all mum wants is for me to feel sorry for her baby daughter. It is all about her nurturing part of maternal love.

Mum does not know that I am infuriated by my sister's attitude towards her. To be fair to my sister, probably she does not know that mum has a fixation on her, being the youngest child in the family. Probably my sister feels uncomfortable that mum is perpetually asking for her. I wish somebody could explain to her that in mum's distorted mind she has gone back fifty or so years back and is now trying to care for her baby girl.

Before mum came to live with me, she lived with my elder sister on the Copper Belt and I remember hearing her fixation on a young man who at the time was living at my sister's house as well (her fixation on this boy must have been triggered by the passing away of mum's youngest son in 2008). However, mum's fixation was misinterpreted and construed into something else. Inappropriate things were said in regards to mum's fixation and things which were said confused mum and as a result, the saga manifested into mum having horrible nightmares and she also started expressing some other difficult behaviours. What mum went through at that time reminds me of an analogy told to me by a very senior lady in an institution where I went to seek some assistance. I kept reminding her of how I had to get back home as soon as possible as the person who assists me to care for mum had to knock off. This lady looked at me and said she also is going through the same problems but she said with her, she has a brother who is equally committed to caring for their mother so the two of them are the sole carers. Then she said her brother had once mentioned to her of a saying that "When a python (very poisonous African snake) grows old and becomes isolated, it bites itself until it dies". I thought of the state I found mum in, she was confused, bitter and extremely angry. What a change, that has taken place within a couple of months, I am not insinuating that mum is not confused nor disoriented but the truth is, presently, mum is much happier and looks much healthier. Would anybody wish their parent to end their life bitter and angry? Of course not, it is just that as human beings we all have our short comings.

Having said so, my elder sister did her best to care for mum and that was in accordance with her affordability. At the same time, there were elements of ignorance in relation to mum's condition. Dementia and caring for the elderly is still under wraps in Zambia and not widely talked about in Zambian communities. There are no discussions on Television nor any mention of funds being released by our government for medicines and care of the elderly. Dementia is still frowned as taboo in most Zambian societies. Sometimes I feel that I am expected to whisper to people when I insist on leaving a meeting or gathering because I have to go and look after my mother who suffers from dementia. I have tried to get any basic prescribed tablets for mum and most times I am hitting against the wall. I am simply utilising my experiences from working as a social worker in England but I am not medical and it hurts me to see mum in pain. Until recently with the help of a stranger, I have managed to find tablets which are calming mum down. She is now much brighter and is able to concentrate on a discussion.

I am putting my thoughts on paper in the hope that somebody will read my notes and probably do something about people who may be facing the same situation as mine. It is time people realised that the chances of an individual growing to a ripe age of (75+) outweighs the chances of one dying from natural causes (I must admit this statistic could be relevant before the ravage onset of HIV & AIDS in the 1980s). Of course this is an individual's opinion and not a researched one.

Mum's un responded love from her children reminds me of an analogy (wise words) quoted on BBC World News one morning which says "When the cock is drunk, it forgets about the bait" Most of us think that one only gets drunk on alcohol or other opiates we forget other intoxicative factors such as power, wealth, love, marriage or hatred. Once one is engulfed in them, nothing else matters until that bubble bursts that's when one reflects back on what is most important to them or what's the most important thing in one's life! A Bemba analogy says, "Mayo mpapa naine nkakupapa" It is about reciprocating parental love! Another Bemba analogy says: "Iyakota yonka mumwana". And for children to ignore an elderly parent is not heard of. Despite, the power, wealth or love one indulges in, there is a cardinal rule which that all of us come from somewhere and that somebody suffered for us to be what we are today!!

However, and based on the same caring subject, one of my nieces commented on her rare visit to my house and while all us were having a chat on how to share caring responsibilities amongst family members, she said "You auntie has been away from Zambia for over thirty years and everybody has moved on in their lives"! I just looked at her (there were other visitors so I did not want to make a nonsense of myself) I thought this girl is very self centred. What has that got to do with caring for your elders. I politely said to her, of course I have been away for a long time for which I do not regret (my migrating from Zambia has made me to be the person I am to-day). However, I reminded this little madam of the fact that after I completed my education/professional studies and acquired a well paid job, I visited Zambia at least twice a year, I sent money and clothes for mum and I also telephoned wherever mum was at least twice a week. Was that not enough care? I asked her. I reminded her that "Moving on" is not abandoning your parent/grand parent to another individual—as this may result in a burnt out syndrome, marriage breakdown or cause a rapid drain on that individual's income. AMEN!!

MUM'S BETRAYAL

IT IS A SUNDAY MORNING. As usual I have no help and I am praying that somebody drops by to help me with the unceasing domestic chores and care for mum. I wake up early around 6.30 am. to give myself enough time to go through a chapter I had typed the previous night—that is, before I start preparing mum for the day.

This Sunday is slightly different because it is not only mum I am caring for, I also have to care for my brother Mr John Jairous Chama whom I had sent for after learning of his serious illness in Samfya District Hospital. He is now recuperating at my house. My brother is a model patient who does not give any hassle but he too needs assistance with bathing, dressing and serving food to him. However, at the time of critical crisis, my male cousin or brother as we refer to 1st cousin in Zambia, Mr Biswell Chimwene came in to assist my brother with transfers, bathing, shaving and dressing. I am indebted to him for his help.

Before midday, I decide to drive into town to pick up a gardener who moors my front lawn. On my way back I pass by my friend's house Ruth whom I hadn't seen for a while as she was away servicing COMESA Meetings in East Africa. Ruth decides to come back with me as she says she wants to see mum.

On my arrival home, I get a phone call from my sister that she is passing by after completing whatever errands she has to do at her new plot. With the help of Ruth, we busy ourselves preparing lunch. Eventually my sister arrives with her son. This pleases mum who sees my sister's visit as a surprise because I had purposely kept my sister's telephone message about her visit secret in case she fails to turn up, a practice which usually upsets mum. Besides, I do not want to spend my Sunday comforting a mother who feels let down by her favourite daughter.

Everybody is happy and joking and there is a very pleasant atmosphere all round. My nephew (my brother's son) also drops in with his friend the house is full of happy people. I am thinking to myself that, this is what I am missing. Having a house full of vivacious, spontaneous happy people. I am used to having all my children and grandchildren on Sunday afternoons when we just chill up, eat, sit and play games, laugh, drink (for those who drink) or merely Basque in the good life of the day.

Whereas, my new life in Zambia is exciting in its own unique way. I find that apart from one or two personal friends I have known since childhood, and one or two of my cousin's children, most family members are vindictive and difficult to get on with. How can family members turn down a memorial dinner for one of their own? In frustration, I gather together my workers (drivers, farm workers, domestic workers and we have a field day). I am always reminded of the Bible story outlined in "Luke 14:16-23".

The most frustrating factor is that at home, I am Living with someone whose conversation is 99% based on her ailments, she does not retain any information hence I cannot hold any reasonable conversation with her. Mum has no clue about the carer's needs. It is not her fault, the mum I know was very caring and she would have been the first person to sympathize and feel sorry for me.

Out of the blue mum goes moody and becomes irritable and agitated. I am trying to figure out the reason why mum should get so upset. Could it be due to the number of people of people in the house. Is it becoming too difficult for her to keep up with the clatter from this excited group of people. Could it be the language barrier? Mum does not speak English. We are all speaking and laughing and mostly the conversation is in English as there are also non-Bemba speaking people around. Having said so, everybody is trying hard to accommodate mum by talking to her in Bemba and bringing her into conversation at any given time. Is she having difficulties in retaining information or she finds our merry mood overwhelming. Or is it lack of attention? Whatever the case, I am loving it. After all anybody needs a break from constant nursing and nurturing of an elderly parent.

However, in the middle of our meal preparation, mum moves into the kitchen where the crowd has now gathered. She starts telling my sister of how she wants to go with her. When my sister queries why she wants to leave, mum says, she feels she has been chased by me. Then she gets excited and starts altering horrible things which have happened to her, such as been locked up in her room while police beat her up. The other one is having been left in a room full of red ants (impashi). She talked of insults being thrown at her. Purportedly all these crimes have been committed by me. My sister did not know where to look or what to say. There is mum urging her to go and pack up all her things so that they leave together. I am standing in front of my cooker making the last dish while taking in all what mum is saying. Ruth is looking at me probably waiting for my reaction.

Momentarily, I am in my own world. I am thinking of what I have given up to look after this un grateful stranger who is cursing me. I go back to my family not knowing what they are eating on this Sunday afternoon. I feel guilty for leaving them and exposing them to being motherless children. I feel a lump rising in my throat. At that very point, I am back with everybody in the kitchen just to hear mum say "make sure you pack all my clothes and leave hers behind". Something snaps in me. I turn round and look at her in surprise. In my mind I am thinking, then you will go with nothing because I have bought all the clothes you have apart from one or two chitenge garments. I always sent or brought clothes for her from England over the years. Outwardly, I say to her, "mum enough is enough" "stop being rude and ridiculous for nothing" "you are spoiling everybody's good time". "If you want to go with your daughter, by all means you may go but stop altering nasty things about me because I am trying my best to care for you". Mum keeps quiet and looks in my sister's direction probably seeking support or expecting her to answer me back. Fortunately she never does. Instead she starts talking to mum about her SDA Service and when mum calms down, she asks mum to go with her to the living room.

I am perplexed with mum's strange behaviours but I keep my cool for I know that she is playing up to seek her baby daughter's attention and pleas. Through guilty or shame, mum strategically refuses to eat her meal until everybody except myself begs and bows before her. Then the woman bounces on her food and eats it to the last drop. I am thinking what is all this fuss about. Why should mum spoil a good day for all of us. Frankly speaking mum's tantrums and strange behaviours on that Sunday afternoon marked a corner stone in my struggle to care for her. For me, a penny had just dropped in front of me. I felt betrayed and used. I felt sorry for myself, I kept thinking, look here Grace, your siblings are getting on with their everyday life, why you are single handedly scratching your head on how best to care for your mum. And now look at how the very woman you care for has turned tables on you in front of everybody.

Incidentally, it did not take long for me to reflect back on mum's previous behaviours at my sister's house. Mum did the same thing and she would go spare accusing my sister and her children of fabricated stories to whoever visited her. That did not go well with me and I used to reprimand her in my sister's presence. And yet my young sister to day ignores the scenario and starts talking to mum as though nothing had happened. The goody goodie type of a person she is.

However, after all visitors leave, I decide to talk to mum in the presence of my elder brother. I sit her down and say, "listen to me mum, I have to face facts with you whenever necessary, I know you suffer from this terrible disease, but sometimes you become yourself and you know what you are talking about". I say to her, "I am not happy with the things you said about me when we were in the kitchen this afternoon". I continued and said "it is not in my nature to live with anybody who dislikes me, may it be a husband, child, mother, sister, brother e.t.c. So if you continue displaying behaviours that you do not like me or start altering false allegations against me to whoever visits you here at my house, I will ask you to LEAVE". Is that clear? Does what I say, make any sense to you? I ask her. My brother keeps quiet and mum looks down. To make sure she understands, I repeat myself to her slowly and finish off by telling her that "what you are doing is betrayal" "Ifi mulecita cikisha cinani" I said, have you heard of that Bemba analogy which goes: The noisy hyena left it's nice hiding place and foolishly exposed itself to it's preditors. "Chimbwi wamufumina, camufumya apasamine, camutwala apaleloka"

My brother does not alter a word. I turn to him and ask: Is there any sense in what I am telling mum? My brother answers and says, yes, there is a lot of sense. My brother says mum should be grateful to you as there is nowhere else where she can go and be looked after the way you do. I thanked my brother and leave the room. By this time, I felt the only way to deal with the frustration and anger inside me was to cry. I went into my bedroom and wept.

A few minutes later, I pull myself together, take a quick shower, pull on a pair of jeans and my old T/shirt and after saying my good byes to mum and my brother, I jump into my pick up vehicle en route to drop fertilizer to workers at the farm. It is at my farm though not fully developed where I feel this strange spiritual calmness, peace and belonging. I love my piece of land, my crops, my animals, chickens, birds (ba kaluku luku and inkunda or doves) and the people who maintain and cultivate it for me.

For me, it is just another day probably slightly different from other Sundays but hey, I am loving it, all the same!!

THE MISSING JEWELLERY BOX

MANY YEARS AGO AND ON one of my regular trips to Zambia, I gave mum my old jewellery box for her to keep her sensitive or important documents like her Zambia National Registration Card, Seventh Day Adventist Christening/Baptism Certificates, her post office book (by then mum was able to go and collect her money from her post office account) old photos e.t.c. Mum has always loved and treasured her jewellery box which she fondly refers to in Bemba as "Akabokoshi".

However while living with mum, I made a short trip to England in August 2011. Mum went to live with my brother in Woodlands, Lusaka. During my absence and whilst living at my brother's house, I was told, a row broke out between mum and my brother over the missing jewellery box.

One morning, mum wakes up in a combat mood after realising that her jewellery box is missing. She decides to confront my brother with multiple incriminating questions. Mum asks my brother: "Akabokoshi kandi mutwele kwisa?" Where have you taken my box? My brother answers her and says, mum you did not come with any box here. Mum retorts back and says you should bring back my box—that's where I keep my SDA Baptism certificates, money and my national registration card. I want my box now! "Ndefwaya Akabokoshi kandi pantu emombika amapepala yabu Docas notukope, elyo ne impiya shandi". My brother casually says to mum, you will find those documents and money when you go back to Makeni. Uugh! goes mum, a sign that she is not happy, somehow she drops the subject but sulks the whole day.

The following morning, mum wakes up with a new twist to her missing box. She decides to go on hunger strike and points out to my brother that she won't eat any of his food until he brings back or finds her missing box. "Ndefwaya Akabokoshi kandi ninshi nefyakulya fyenu nshyalyeko pano pa ng'nda iyoo. My brother is alarmed by mum's overwhelming reactions to her missing box. He quietly picks up the phone and starts making inquiries from people who might know the whereabouts of mum's jewellery box. His first call goes to Anne (my niece who is mum's paid carer) Anne says she has no idea of the whereabouts of her grandmother's box. My brother next telephones my young sister on the copper belt who also denies any knowledge of the box in question. My brother reports once more to mum that after making various inquiries nobody seems to know where her jewellery box is. Mum sneers at him and says "Muno mung'anda nafula sana pali umo uwibile akabokashi kandi". (You are so many in this house and one of you has stolen my jewellery box). My brother swallows hard and leaves mum after telling her that his children can not steal her jewellery box as it's contents would not interest them. Mum, who usually likes to put in her last word retorts back and says, there is a lot of money in her jewellery box (referring to U.S. $10 or $20 equivalent). Anyway my brother leaves and vows to look for mum's jewellery box. Somehow my brother decides not to mention the missing jeweller box to his children nor his wife for fear of repercussions and general destabilization of his household. He then reports back to mum and says, nobody I have spoken to knows the where about of the jewellery box you are talking about.

A few days later, mum who is already agitated vents out her anger on him and retorts back at him by viciously sneering at him by saying: "Muno mung'anda mulibengi sana elyo pabana bobe pali umo uwibile Akabokoshi kandi". (There are a lot of you in this house and probably one of your children has stolen my jewellery box). My brother is got-smacked. He tries to reason with mum that none of his children have any knowledge of her box and besides none of them has ever stolen anything from this house.

However, on my return back home, my brother decides to pay us unexpected visit at my house in Makeni. At the same time, my brother feels uncomfortable and frustrated over mum's accusations of the missing jewellery box. He feels uncomfortable and very frustrated. He knows such accusations may cause problems between him and his wife who may not like to think that her children are prime suspects in her in-laws missing box. Anyway my brother keeps his agonising thoughts to himself and does not tell the children nor the wife about the missing box. Somehow he manages to coax mum into abandoning her self imposed fasting and she readily resumes eating her meals.

Knowing my mother's current temperaments and her accusations, I believe my brother must have promised to replace the missing box or promised to refund the money for mum to agree eating food from his house and to get the subject dropped there and then.

However, on mum's return from Woodlands, she found her jewellery box sitting and waiting for her where she had left it, in her wardrobe. One day my brother called round my flat unexpectedly and as usual he strides in the house and goes straight into mum's bedroom. He knocks and opens the door, he likes surprising mum with his unexpected arrivals. He finds mum sitting on her bed, busy going through her jewellery box. My brother could not believe what he was seeing. My brother later told me that for a brief moment, he just stood watching mum's actions. He said, mum was sitting on her bed clenching her jewellery box probably trying to hide it from him or better still protecting it from him.

My brother could not believe what he was seeing. He goes near to mum and asks, mum what are you holding in your hands, didn't I tell you that you had left your jewellery box in Makeni? By the way, what was that fussy of you accusing me and my children of stealing your box? Mum who is found red handed but wouldn't admit her wrong accusation nor apologize counter reacts and starts accusing my brother for not packing the jewellery box when he fetched her from Makeni. In mum's words she says: "Kabili nimwe mwalongele ifipe fyandi elyo mwasha aka bokoshi". (You are the one who packed my belongs and left out my jewellery box). My brother couldn't believe mum cannot have the courtesy of saying sorry but instead she jumps to self defence. He decides to drop the subject, still fuming he comes to the kitchen where I was and starts telling me the events of the day when my mum accused him and his children of stealing her jewellery box and how he has just found mum sitting on her bed clenching the box with other papers scattered on her bed. I advised my brother between fits of laughter that mum's pastime activity is going through her jewellery box counting and re-arranging contents of her open jewellery box. My brother just stands there not believing what he had just witnessed. I also informed him that after mum counts her loot, and depending on what she finds in the box, she either accuses carers or owner of the house (myself) of removing or stealing money from the box.

Somehow, my brother backs out of the room and walks to the kitchen where I was. He had this funny look on his face that I immediately asked him what had gone wrong. He said in fits of laughter that he had just caught mum sitting on her bed going throw the contents of her jewellery box which she had reported missing at his house. I started laughing with him and I assured my brother that mum might have even forgotten that she made such accusations. We both agreed that mum's stunned look might have been due to her fear for having somebody enter her room unexpectedly which she perceived as intrusion into her privacy. I informed my brother that mum has labelled me a thief in my own house so many times and that it has reached a point where I no longer get upset over such accusations.

However, still in fits of laughter I turn to my brother and inquire whether mum had apologised to him over the false allegations. My brother wipes laughter induced tears from his eyes. And says mum was stunned and she blankly looked at me without altering a word. My brother looks straight at me and says, "No, aren't you aware of the fact that there is no saying 'sorry to your own child' in mum's generation" Then he goes, don't we say 'The customer is always right' or 'The Boss is always right' so in mum's generation 'The parent is always right'. Then we burst out laughing.

Within a few minutes we hear mum's stamp, stamp noises from her walking stick. I hastily whisper to my brother that mum is coming to investigate what we are laughing at and she will get upset if she knows we are laughing at her. So we stand still awaiting her arrival. Immediately we saw her enter the kitchen we started flattering her.

Oh dear, there comes mum who is intrigued by our noises of laughter. I am secretly nodding at my brother to stop laughing because if mum guesses we are laughing at her supposedly missing jewellery box she will get agitated so we both behave ourselves and start talking to mum over her favourite subjects, namely her ailments and grandchildren.

Oh mum likes excessive attention being paid to her. She felt and appeared happy. She later started telling us about her unceasing illnesses. Nobody has ever mentioned anything about her missing jewellery box again.

THE GRACE PASSAGE

As EARLIER EXPLAINED IN PREVIOUS chapters, I migrated from Zambia to England in the late 1970s.

With hind sight, I perceive myself as being lucky in that my departure from Zambia was not due to my own hard work nor any academic/professional achievements, I followed my husband who had been sponsored to study accountancy in England. Probably I had made a mark in the short period I had been married to my husband who, in appreciation approached his employers to arrange for my passage and our two little boys to join him in England. Probably my lucky passage could correctly be termed as a pillow merit?

Legend has it that his work colleague who was awarded same accountancy scholarship never invited his family to join him in England. It was also reported that on this individual's return back to Zambia, after a couple of years living alone in England, he divorced the very woman whom he had left behind to endure veracious hardships on her own with the man's children.

On reflection, my husband and other bright young Zambians were among the lucky ones who enjoyed Zambia's honeymoon after Independence. The scholarships were raining in doves enabling any bright young man and woman who wanted to pursue his/her career in various academic and professional fields to do so through their employers or government bursaries.

Unlike these days, when young men and women fleeing economic hardships and civil wars in their countries flood the western world thereby making the world view Africa as mother continent of economic refugees, Zambian sponsored students received overseas allowances, which included tuition fees, accommodation or boarding fees, spouse allowances and in addition, continued to receive their salaries in Zambia. Boy! those were days when being a wife of a sponsored student was something to be proud of.

However, Zambia's rugs to riches story was enhanced by various factors such as civil wars in neighbouring countries. Unlike current war fare, in the 1960s, 1970s and 1980s wars in Africa were fought using fire arms loaded with copper bullets. This coincided with the booming ship building as well as electronics industries in Europe, Japan and the far east which depended on copper rods. Zambia was then accredited the third largest copper producer in the world. I remember being so big-headed, pompous and cheeky with anybody who poked racist fun at me. The common one being "Where on earth do you come from?" As though his or her question is not clear to me. The cheek would continue and ask: "Do you come from

Jamaica?" I would bark back and say, "I do not come from Jamaica". Not accepting defeat, the cheek goes on with: "Do you come from Nigeria?" In my heart I would sneer and say so in your racist ignorant, small mind anybody with a black skin comes from either Jamaica or Nigeria! But to the racist I would shout back and say, I do not come from Nigeria either. The cheek continues and says "where do you come from then?" I just swallow hard and put on a very strong, exaggerated cracking African accent and say, "I cumee frome Zambia" Undeterred the cheek continues and annoyingly sneers at me and says, "where is Zambia?" Then I turn nasty and sneer back and say, "Did you go to school? The cheek looks straight at me and says "Yes I did". Then I sarcastically make a slur between my teeth and say, "Then your geography must have been next to nothing", and I add on and say "Zambia is the third largest copper producer in the World" and on that note I would walk or majestically Clyde away" Guess what? The following day when I bump into this red neck in another lecture, he beckons to me and says, "Hey, you come from a very rich country, what does your father do? I give him a big smile and say "My father owns a copper mine" He goes "Whaah, Whaah, Whaah." I just walk away laughing my head off. For starters, I feel satisfied that the cheek went to the library to research on Zambia (this was late eighties before google internet searches). Secondly the cheek will respect me for being a rich woman. After all, how could he know that my father is in fact dead and that he was merely an ex mine policeman in Zambian colonial era. Coming to think about survival in a foreign territory, who can dispute the fact that sometimes a white lie works wonders.

Coming back to my grace passage, I vividly remember travelling to London on 17th February, 1977 accompanied by my two little boys aged three and one and half years. I had no Visa except for my air tickets, those days one does not need to get a visa in Lusaka. The visa was being issued on arrival in the United Kingdom. Immigration or Customs officers fetched me on arrival at Heathrow Airport. They kept warning me of the severe cold weather and inquired if I had brought any warm clothing for the children. I opened my hand language and pulled out two children's coats which their father had already sent to Zambia in readiness for the trip. Afterwards, the female customs officer knelt down and started putting coats on my little boys.

I quietly congratulated myself and thought, YES! I have reached England, a land of PLENTY, A LAND OF RICHES, A LAND OF KNOWLEDGE, A LAND WHERE RICHES AND HARMONY FORM UNCEASING PARTNERSHIP. Little did I know, that I would soon put my tail between my legs and stick to my in-born label of "a black person in a Whiteman's land". Are we black? I kept asking my husband, I think we are brown. My husband would just laugh and say, this is not Zambia, people in this country do not look at colour pigmentation, anybody who is not white is black no matter how light skinned one is, even mixed race individuals are referred to as black people.

On reflection, and writing about it now, I must confess I hated the term "black". Incidentally, I had to accept and live with it and in later years, especially after passing through University I became very proud of being referred to as a "black person". To me, being black meant and still means being tough tested, an achiever a persistent person, who endures to make any gains through blood sweat. My slogan has since changed to "nothing is impossible to a black person".

Remember I arrived in England in the late 1970s and racism and it's brutal ethos was at it's highest levels. Have you heard of Notices for houses or rooms for rent in England which read "No blacks, No Dogs and No Irish" This period was marked by various political racist speeches such as those given by Enock Powell, Norman Tebbitt and many other Conservative politicians. Political Elections were won by waving racist cards. That was then, and it is benefiting to say such tensions have since eased and the World has witnessed the rise in black people holding positions of power both in politics and private sectors in the Western World.

Coming back to my arrival at Heathrow Airport, the Immigration officers invited me and my children to sit on a chair and asked me to wait while they went to fetch my husband from where he was waiting for us. Can you imagine a wife of a student getting such VIP treatment at London's Heathrow Airport these days? However, after the normal formalities we left Heathrow Airport en route to Birmingham in the West Midlands and for me that marked my arrival in my new adopted country which I fondly refer to as my "father country". Great Britain has embraced my economical, financial and educational needs while Zambia is my "mother country" which provides and meets my spiritual, social and nurturing needs. Thankfully, both countries are very dear to me and have equally contributed to my well being in their own separate ways.

Life in England was fine until my husband's sponsorship came to an abrupt end before completion of his studies. As a young couple with two boys and a new baby girl we had no option but to return back home to Zambia. After a spell of a couple of years life became even harder for us hence my husband had to convince another sponsor within Zimco Group of Companies to enable him to go and complete his accountancy studies. Luckily enough he was once more sent abroad and a year later I followed with the children. This time round and based in London itself I started looking for a job. One temporary secretarial job led to more permanent ones.

During my spare time especially over weekends I used to type assignments/thesis for various overseas students. This was the time when computer technology burst on the market. I bought myself an AMSTRAD computer and my private typing was booming. By then my husband's sponsorship had once more been discontinued. Have you heard of an analogy which is common among foreign students that accountancy studies can take up to fifteen years to complete and the person studying becomes a "professional student" never finishing studies but always being argumentative, negative and critical of other people especially those excelling in their line of study. Luckily for my family, my private income and a day's job enabled my husband to attend and continue with his studies while children excelled in primarily and junior schools. We lived well and a few years later, my husband managed to pass both ACCA and SIMA final papers. Brilliant chap he was! He had caved himself a career as a qualified accountant!

Whoo! Whoo! Little did I know that the fact that he no longer depended on my income marked the end of a loving and caring relationship and started a rather practical grinding and rusty existence with a lot of don'ts! My husband forged new slogans such as "a woman's place is in the kitchen", "don't answer back when I am talking to you woman"! Whoo! Whoo! Whoo!

However, one evening while going through typed papers with a West African PhD female student, I got a surprise of my life. She made a proposal which I had quietly been spinning on but was not brave enough to voice it out. I will call the PhD lady Nancy, because I have forgotten her name although I feel she was Nancy. Anyway, Nancy stood up and stretched herself and asked where my husband was. I said I am not sure, he could be with friends I responded. I looked at her and asked why she was asking me about my husband? She firmly said, because I want to talk to you about something and I do not want your husband to know about our discussion.

I stopped what I was doing and looked at her suspiciously. What does this woman want to talk about I thought. What has she been told about my husband? A million things went through my head and when I recovered I weakly said to her, go on then, what do you want to tell me? Nancy looked at me and said, Grace have you got any future aspirations? I said, what do you mean? She said, "have you ever thought about advancing yourself professionally" By now, I am secretly cursing her, I am thinking I am alright mate, the fact that you are pursuing a PhD Degree does not entitle you to go round recruiting wives and mothers into going back to school.

Outwardly, I used my usual escapism charm and laughed out loudly. Nancy looked at me and said, "stop laughing Grace. You're such a talented woman you need to do something better for yourself". Alright then, I said to her, what can I do, I am married and I have four children. Nancy looked at me and I saw fury in her eyes. She then sat down and said. Look here, my dear, I am a married woman too, my husband is back home in West Africa with our six children. I have reached this far through a big struggle. And look, she said, I am forty eight years old and you are still in your early thirties. Don't loose this opportunity while you are here in England. You are a very clever woman who can cave out a very meaningful career for yourself.

I just sat there dumb folded and feeling stupid. Two things dawned on me. Firstly, I thought of how belittled I felt each time my husband's fellow students visited home. I could quickly retreat into the kitchen and start preparing meals afraid of joining in their conversations (professional debates as they were deemed). I sometimes envied them and desperately wanted to fully participate in their discussions but my husband always reminded me that I was not educated enough to understand such debates at a professional level—what! loud and challenging discussions which usually started with ACCA/SIMA equations and ended up with Zambian politics. What couldn't I understand? For all good reasons, what my husband meant was that I had no degree all I had were secretarial certificates and diplomas under my belt.

I was in a stupor because to me in that split second I reflected back to a similar incident in 1973 when after cutting short my teacher training course at then Kwame Nkhruma College in Kabwe, I started applying for clerical jobs in the civil service. I got a positive response from the Ministry of Finance and after preliminary selection tests, I was sent with other chosen candidates to go and see a Mr Siame at Tender Board where we underwent further written and verbal interviews. After the interviews, Mr Siame called me to his office. My heart was in my mouth, as I thought of a million things which might have gone wrong during the precarious interviews. However, Mr Siame sat me down and asked his secretary to fetch me drinking water. He fished out my papers from the pile he had and asked, "Did you go to Kasama Girls Secondary School? I answered back "Yes Sir", then he asked, Did you know a girl called Rosby Namwila? I said "Yes Sir" she was my senior. In fact she was two years my senior. Then Mr Siame said, that is my sister. When I look at you I feel like I am looking at my sister why are wasting time applying for clerical jobs when you have such good results? Why didn't you go to University? I had to think fast, as I debated whether I should tell this stranger the truth or not. I thought to myself no, no, the truth won't suffice, I should say something more convincing. I looked up and said, my father passed away and there would not have been anybody to pay the

University fees. I continued and said, I also want to get a job so that I may assist my young brothers and sister with their education. Yes my father passed away but that is not the reason why I left teacher training college nor did not go to University. Well, on this episode, my white lie worked as I saw Mr Siame pick up the phone and started talking to somebody on the other end, whom I later learnt was the Principal at Evelyn College. He casually said, "I have a brilliant candidate for your courses there, I have asked her to come and see you tomorrow". Then he turned to me and said, "You did very well in your interviews but I am not giving you this clerical job, you should go to Evelyn Hone College and enrol on a secretarial course.

As I was preparing to stand up and leave his office, Mr Siame said, by the way "the course started a week ago, I am sure you will catch up". After which he started writing something on a piece of paper which he folded and put in an envelop. He handed the envelop to me and said, take this letter to the Principal at Evelyn Hone College tomorrow morning. In the meantime I will talk to him and he will be expecting you. I took the envelop and said "Thank You Very Much" and left Mr Siame's office. Little did I know, that, this man, I hardly knew opened the doors to my entire World. The rest is history.

There was something so special about Mr Siame. He was so calm and reassuring! He had that poignant presence! The finale spotter! A man of integrity and authority! The Old School Type! Those twenty or thirty minutes I spent in his office, which had an oval table with red or green velvet lining around it are still vivid in my head thirty eight or so years latter. How could he spot and help a stranger just like that? All I can say to Mr Siame or his spirit is that you installed one value which I have carried on—wherever I am, or whatever I am doing, in work or business, I am forever helping people who are vulnerable and less fortunate than me.

However, after many, many years through fate I met and knew Zipora Simuzhya, who happened to be Mr Siame's niece. I told her my strange encounter with her uncle and I pleaded with her that she leads me to meet her auntie, "Ba Roby" whom Zipora said visits her at her shop. And for sure, one morning while lazing around at my sister's uniform shop which was next door to Zipro's and Ba Rosby came along. We had a good chat about Kasama Girls and she further told me that she had gone to the University of Zambia and majored in Education. She told me she had taught in so many secondary schools and that she is now retired. When I inquired about her brother Mr Siame of Tender Board, Ba Rosby told me that Mr Siame passed away. I just walked away. When I got to the place where I was staying I just broke down and wept. I wanted to meet that man and thank him and tell him how he had put me in the right direction. I wanted him to know that after Evelyn Hone College, I had held very senior secretarial positions in both civil service, private sector and even worked at UNDP and PTA now COMESA before I left for United Kingdom. Mr Siame gave me a priceless gift and he will forever remain my HERO. MHSRIP!

And now this PhD student has spotted something in me. Is it true that history repeats itself? I am now silently psyching myself, I jerk myself and say, Grace think quickly, this woman can help you, stop going over what happened to you in Zambia concentrate and entice this woman into explaining to you on how to apply for a University place. Then I said to Nancy, Ok, that sounds like a good idea, how do I apply for a University place. Nancy said you write or ring UCAS the governing body for University Clearing Body in England and Wales. I said alright then, I will see what I can do about it. Nancy goes, don't just see: but do something about it. That is how our discussion ended and we got back to correcting her papers.

A few months latter I managed to secure both a place at the University and a Grant from my Local Authority which covered tuition and living allowances throughout my four years' study. I enrolled at University. Four years later, I majored with flying colours and attained a B.A. Sociology degree with a Certificate of Qualified Social Workers. I then embarked on a Social Worker's career which brought me a lot of dignity and happiness.

Now the question arises, where is Nancy? I have no idea, frankly speaking, I do not know. She could be a doctor of philosophy anywhere in the World but I always think about her and thank her for her courage in approaching me and putting me once more in the right direction. It is a small world, one day, I will meet that clever woman with A BIG HEART!!!

GLOSSARY

Ati shani	—	What or what are you saying
Aada	—	Oh, no, or tell me about it!
Neebo	—	Me
Uuugh	—	Expression of dissatisfaction/disapproval
Ifwe	—	We or plural of me
Akapiya	—	money
Akabokoshi	—	Box
Akalimba	—	Radio/television
Inama	—	Meat
Isabi	—	Fish
Umusalu	—	Vegetables
Ifimisalu	—	Plural for vegetables especially the ones she dislikes
Kabiki	—	Cabbage
Inkoto	—	Walking stick
Icifunga	—	Skirt
Indeleshi	—	Dress
Ishati	—	Shirt/blouse/top
Utumenshi	—	Water
Utwakaba	—	Hot water
Utwatalala	—	Cold water
Imbwa	—	Dog
Awee mukwai	—	Leave me alone
Ukusingula	—	Painting
Umunani	—	Relish
Umucele	—	Salt

Shuka	—	Sugar
Findo/Finshi	—	What
Iwe/Webo/Imwe	—	You
Ine	—	Me
Umukashi	—	Pair of scissors
Buleti/Umukate	—	Bread
Nafwa	—	I am dead
Mutulee	—	Help
Natemwa	—	I am happy
Kateka	—	President

RESUME

Grace Chama-Pupe (nee') Grace Chama Katebe was born on 28th December, 1952 in Chief Mulala Area, Luwingu District, in Northern Province of Zambia.

She was the sixth child in a family of nine in which three babies perished in their infancy and only six survived into adulthood. However, this number was further reduced to five in 2008 when the eighth boy passed away at the age of 50.

At the age of 12, Grace was selected to attend the prestigious Chipili Girls Boarding School which was run by White Anglican Missionaries near Mansa in Luapula Province of Zambia.

After primary education, Grace attended Kasama Girls Secondary School in Northern Province of Zambia where she obtained 8 'O' Levels.

In 1973, Grace enrolled at Evelyn Hone College to pursue a secretarial Course. After a brief high profile secretarial career in Zambia, Grace immigrated to the United Kingdom in 1977. Whilst in United Kingdom, Grace pursued a four year degree course and attained a Bachelor of Arts in Sociology, and a Certificate of Qualified Social Workers (CQSW) qualification. She further attained a Diploma in Community and Primary Health Care (Dip. CPHC).

Married and a mother of four, Grace worked as a Social Worker in various London Local Authorities. However, she returned back to her native Zambia in February, 2011. The unexpected responsibility left on her to care and look after her widowed mother who suffers from onset dementia led her to writing a book detailing her everyday frustrations as well as exciting moments with her elderly mother.

Grace today, is a proud mother of four adult children and four grandchildren. She readily admits that she now lives in two countries as she divides her time between nursing her mother in Zambia and making frequent visits to her family back in the United Kingdom.

Printed in Great Britain
by Amazon.co.uk, Ltd.,
Marston Gate.